Praise for *Losing Wonder Woman*

Authenticity ain't got nothing on Kermit Farmer. This book is a prescription for courage, fortitude, and love.

— **Matthew Zachary**, Cancer Survivor and
Host of "Out of Patients" Podcast

In "Losing Wonder Woman", Kermit Farmer has given us an incredible look at the power of faith, family, and fight. The story of real-life superhero, the cancer doctor-turned-patient Linda Farmer, is inspiring, heartbreaking, and leads us to hope even in the hardest moments imaginable. Linda was my friend and colleague, and because of Kermit's book, I'm still learning from her.

— **W. Lee Warren**, MD Host of The Dr. Lee Warren Podcast
and award-winning author of Hope Is the First Dose

Losing Wonder Woman is a beautiful and poignant memoir. In true Kermit form, this is a "love tsunami" written for his wife, son, and all those who hear the unimaginable news of a cancer diagnosis. It is also his "pufferfish" path of service that carries on the legacy of his special Wonder Woman.

— **Barbara Alvarez Martin**, DrPH, MPH, Cancer survivor and an assistant
director of a NCI-designated comprehensive cancer center

As Kermit pens his path through the grieving process to healing, he provides hope, wisdom and purpose, leveraging his loss for the benefit of us all and honoring the all-too-often undervalued caregivers of the world along the way.

– **Topher Willkins**, Executive Director of Opportunity Collaboration and Community Builder

Kermit Farmer's poignant book, "Losing Wonder Woman," is a heartfelt tribute to his wife, Linda, whose compassionate spirit and unwavering dedication as an oncologist touched countless lives. Through Farmer's eloquent storytelling, readers are immersed in Linda's world, where her love for others, particularly her patients, shines brightly amidst the darkness of illness and despair.

In the face of adversity, Linda's empathy knew no bounds. Farmer vividly portrays her remarkable ability to offer solace and support, even when facing her own struggles. Whether comforting a young woman abandoned by her spouse or lending a comforting hand to a frightened patient, Linda's compassion knew no limits. Her genuine care and steadfast presence created a sense of belonging and hope for those in their darkest moments.

Farmer beautifully captures Linda's reliance on faith and the profound impact it had on her approach to medicine. Through prayer and devotion, she found strength beyond herself, guiding her through the challenges of her profession with grace and determination. Her faith wasn't merely a personal comfort but a source of power that infused her interactions with patients, offering them a sense of peace and resilience in their own battles.

"Losing Wonder Woman" is more than a memoir; it's a testament to the enduring legacy of a remarkable woman whose love knew no bounds. Farmer's words resonate with authenticity and deep emotion, inviting readers to celebrate Linda's life and the profound impact she made on those around her. This book is a stirring reminder of the power of compassion, faith, and love in the face of adversity, inspiring readers to embrace these virtues in their own lives."

– **Lee Hicks,** Bestselling Author, Public Speaker, Healthcare IT, & CEO

LOSING
Wonder
WOMAN

LOSING
Wonder
WOMAN

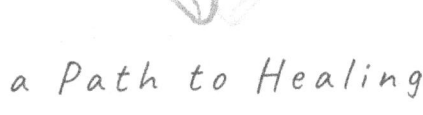

a Path to Healing

Kermit Farmer

STONE CREST

STONE CREST
www.stonecrestbooks.com

Stone Crest Publishing www.stonecrestbooks.com

Losing Wonder Woman © Copyright 2024 Kermit Farmer
First Edition

Published in the United States by Stone Crest Books
Stone Crest Books | www.stonecrestbooks.com
An imprint of Dinosaur House

ISBN: 978-1-961462-21-2 (hardcover)
        978-1-961462-22-9 (paperback)
        978-1-961462-23-6 (ebook)

Executive Editor: Paul Fair
Publishing Manager: Stone Crest Books

This book is dedicated to my North Star, to my son Spencer Kermit Farmer and to the 19,000 + former patients under my wife's care in their cancer journey.

This book is also dedicated to the front line of healthcare workers that includes those who find balance in life and those suffering from moral injury described in this book.

And finally, it is dedicated to the caregivers of the world. You are the invisible faces hiding in plain sight, providing love and support 24/7 and sometimes with no end in sight. Your work is supported. Your work is seen here.

A special shout out to my editors Andrea and Nancy and Kayla for making me look so good. It takes a village to keep me straight.

TABLE OF CONTENTS

Prologue..1

Linda's Family Tree 5

Part I..7

    Chapter 1 – I Married Wonder Woman...9

    Chapter 2 – "Find a Way to Keep Dr. Farmer"....................................31

    Chapter 3 – A Closet, an Oath, and Moral Injury 45

    Chapter 4 – Hurry Up and Wait 57

    Chapter 5 – The Spencer Cancer Center 75

Part II 89

    Chapter 6 – The Cancer Doctor Gets Cancer.......................................91

    Chapter 7 – I Can't Carry Your Cancer, But I Can Carry You...........101

    Chapter 8 – The Wound That Never Heals..117

    Chapter 9 – 18 Days 133

    Chapter 10 – It's OK To Not Be OK..151

    Chapter 11 – "Who Lives, Who Dies, Who Tells Your Story?".........167

Acknowledgements 175

About The Author 177

A Path For All 179

PROLOGUE

*M*ake sure to get the dogs their food," Linda says, patting her dog Jordan sitting beside her, "Sometimes you forget about that." I nod along, adding "dogs" to my mental list that was already growing beyond my ability to remember. *I'm sure she'll leave a written list for me somewhere,* I think as I get up from the bed. Months prior to this moment, I ordered an adjustable bed for us. That bed was split down the middle, with separate twin beds pushed together to raise and decline independently. To see Linda, I flipped my bed around and raised it to a forty-five-degree angle, just like hers. We looked like the grandparents from *Willy Wonka & the Chocolate Factory.*

I walk to the bathroom and open the cabinet, fumbling through Linda's medicine. "And you have to make sure Spencer gets a good education," I hear from the other room. I add "Spencer" to the list for the fourth, or maybe the fifth, time. "You have to instill that in him. He's thick-headed, you know." I chuckle, knowing that to be true. Whatever gift Linda has for academics, she did not pass it along to our son. That boy is smart in every other aspect, but mathematics (his mom's favorite) is not his strong suit.

"Anything else?" I ask from the bathroom.

"Yes," Linda says from the bed, "Let's talk about you."

"About me?" I close my eyes for a moment then poke my head around the corner. She's facing away from me, but I can see she's referencing a list in her lap. *So, there is a written list. I knew it.*

"Yes, we need to talk about your next steps, when I'm not going to be here," she says, waving me over. I sigh, already anticipating this to be a beautifully uncomfortable conversation. She looks at me with a knowing grin and all I can do is muse at her ever-present practicality. I take a deep breath and let it out as I crawl into my side of the bed for the thirtieth time that day.

1

"I've been thinking," she says, tapping the pen to her chin, "You can begin to date a year after I pass."

Oh, here we go. "Linda—" I try to interrupt.

"And you're welcome to get married two years after," she says, looking me deadpan in the face.

Resolute but still soft.

"Linda, we're not going to talk about this—"

"Well, there's nothing left to talk about," she says, clicking her pen as a way to end the conversation.

My jaw hangs loose behind my closed lips, and I stammer out, "But I—Well, you are impossible. Ugh!" *Dammit woman.*

We share a look. *This is so Linda.* "Do you have anything else for me from your little notepad?" I say, leaning back to look up at the ceiling.

"You have to take care of yourself. You don't hydrate enough. I've seen your pee."

"Alright, alright, alright," I say, my face getting hot. I look to Linda, who's smiling a bit now, too. Even in her last days, she still enjoys making me a honey-do list. "Anything else?" I ask, despite being afraid of what she could possibly say next. She shakes her head, returning her attention back to the notepad.

I nod, bringing my eyes back to the ceiling. I know she isn't *trying* to make this conversation as difficult as possible. It's just *Linda.* Like when she ransacks the house looking for the one sock that goes missing after pulling the clothes from the dryer. My girl, the oncologist, "Dr. Farmer," needs things complete, and things done right. In her mind, this is the best way she knows how to go. Not leaving any stone unturned, or any wrong not righted. I can't fault her for that, and honestly, I expect nothing less.

I move closer to gently sit in the space next to her, careful not to jostle her too much. She looks up at me, and smiles.

"There's going to be a lot of casseroles showing up at our house once I'm gone. There's a lot of single girls out there, you know. And you like to cook,"

2

she says, preparing me for what she suspects will be some zombie horde of women banging on our door while holding freshly baked casseroles.

"You've got to be prepared for that. You can't just accept any woman's casserole."

"Alright, my love. . . ."

LINDA'S FAMILY TREE

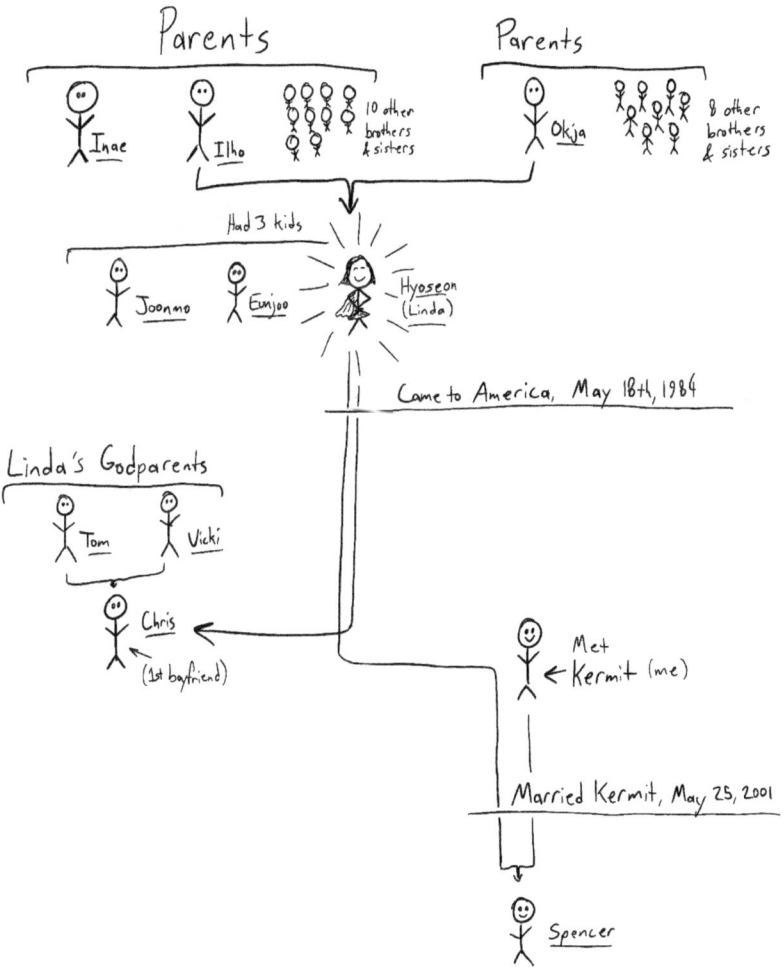

PART I

CHAPTER 1

I Married Wonder Woman

"What's your name?"
"Hyoseon Lee."

The immigration officer's eyebrows shot up half an inch. He leaned forward. "What was that? 'Hi-sen'?!"

"No. Hi-yo-sen," the girl repeated, standing in front of the man's desk. Though fifteen years old, she looked closer to twelve. She wore a light blue dress that hung from her shoulders, and her socks sagged around her bony ankles. She looked at her father and mother behind her, who spoke even less English than she did, then to her aunt just behind them, who nodded at her encouragingly. She turned back to the officer and repeated slowly, emphasizing her breath on the H:

"Hi. Yo. Sen," she repeated, with a pause between each syllable.

The officer turned from the girl to the translator, shrugged, then looked back. "That's not going to work. Can you pick something else? Do you have a nickname?"

She watched the translator, nodding. A new name. She thought for a minute, then asked, "What is Wonder Woman name?" she asked in Korean. The two men blinked in unison.

"Um, it's Lynda Carter. I think," the translator said.

She nodded, a tiny smile on her lips. "Call me Linda."

I'm convinced my wife, Linda Lee, came out of the womb a badass. Made of pure grit and unyielding determination. Perhaps if she'd been born at a different time, she would have been some combination of Lucy Liu and Lynda Carter, with the cut-throat intensity of the *Kill Bill* assassin (barring a tendency for violence) and the candor and kindness of Wonder Woman. But if there was one quality that surpassed even her badass-ness, it was her selflessness. A quality so deeply rooted in love, it was dangerous. Not to others, but to herself, made from the same Love that got a man killed on a Roman tree two millennia ago.

But let's not get too far ahead.

It was 1970 in South Korea. Linda was born to the name, Hyoseon Lee, the third child to a gambling alcoholic and eventual pig farmer. When her father, Ilho, turned twenty, he'd been lucky enough to marry Linda's mother, the true source of both brains and heart in the family. Ilho was the youngest of eight children born to a wealthy father. If Ilho needed a house, he got a house. If he needed money, he got money. When I asked Linda's aunt, Ilho's older sister, about him, she said he wasn't a bad person, despite being an alcoholic (at least he was never an *angry* alcoholic); he was just spoiled.[1]

Linda's mother, Ilho's wife, Okja, was the silent yet sturdy backbone of the family. As any good Korean housewife was expected to do, she obeyed Ilho, listened to his direction, and at the end of the day, respected his decisions. Even the bad ones. But on the hard days, she relied on something far greater.

Okja was introduced to Christ by her sister, and from that day on, God became the source of her strength and purpose. She taught her three children, Eunjoo, Joonmo, and Hyoseon of Jesus's sacrifice and resurrection, and of the hope and peace to be found in God's will over their own. Okja showed them what it looked like to give thanks in their deficit, offer praise in the middle of their struggles, and find contentment in whatever life circumstance they were in. Linda clung to these teachings from an early age, finding strength in the hope they provided.

---

[1] I preferred "scoundrel" but I went with Aunt Inae's kinder description.

When Linda was five years old, Ilho's father passed, leaving Ilho an ample sum of money. Within two years, it was squandered on games, bets, and alcohol. The Lee family was then destitute.

About this time, Ilho's sister Inae (the real black sheep of the family, at least according to their father) came to visit from America, the "place of opportunity." She had done the worst thing a Korean could ever do ... marry an American. Worse, an American *soldier*.

They met in 1953. Inae was working at the ground base as a secretary when she met Bob. Within a few weeks, they fell in love with each other (all without her knowing a lick of English, nor him any Korean) and decided to get married. Inae was willing to risk being shunned by her family to live the life she wanted. After the wedding, they packed up and moved to Japan after promising Ilho to come back to visit South Korea once their father was gone. By 1957, they'd settled in America where Inae learned to speak English. There, she was able to raise her son in peace. Eighteen years later, their father passed. She was finally able to visit her home and family in South Korea.

On her visit, Inae sat across from her brother Ilho while the children played on the floor, taking turns with the new toy she'd brought them. "You should come to America," she urged Ilho. "The kids can have a proper education, go to university like my son. Think of their future. And—" she said, looking over at Okja with sympathetic eyes, "think of your wife." Ilho nodded, looking at Okja, who'd been sick on and off. "I will consider," he said. It was 1975.

Five years later, the Lee family was still in South Korea. Ilho had scrounged up enough money to buy a pig farm. All the children worked the farm for Ilho; Linda's job was to feed the pigs. Every day for three years, Linda took care of pigs before and after school. She showed up at school always fearful of literally smelling like a pig. With ragged stained clothes, and hair she tried to comb back as much as possible, she did her best to ignore the other students' jeers and whispers. But the face of poverty is hard to disguise. She remembered what her mother taught her years before and continued to pray: "God's will is greater than our own; walk in faith, treating others with love and kindness." She let most jibes roll off her shoulders, and what insults she couldn't defend only hardened her resolve to outsmart those around her. She told herself she was going to be the best. And she was.

That same year, 1983, Ilho lost the farm, and finally picked up the phone to call Aunt Inae. It took another year for the paperwork to get shuffled to the right desk, stamped by the right people, and finally approved. By 1984, the Lee family was on the plane heading for America, sponsored by the First Baptist Church in Winston-Salem, North Carolina.

Linda looked out her window and saw the Statue of Liberty. It looked like the picturesque American dream. It told her everything she needed to know about her new home. To the world, Lady Liberty symbolizes peace and opportunity. But for Linda, it also signaled education. From the moment she stepped onto American soil, she was going to *learn*. Learn English. Learn Science. Learn *America*.

I was twenty-nine when I first met Linda in 2000. Each morning and afternoon, I would walk my chow from my apartment to the dog park down the hill. Sometimes I'd see this gargantuan beast of a golden retriever dragging along this skinny, just over five-foot tall, dark-haired Asian woman. The first time, I remember chuckling at the sight. Then, I started to feel bad for the woman. Or maybe she was a teenager. I couldn't tell from where I stood, but what I did know was that that dog was out of control, and this poor person was struggling. I couldn't help but look down at my stately, disciplined, somewhat regal chow and laugh at the irony. While my six-foot-two shadow engulfed that of my chow, this Asian woman's golden retriever was practically walking her. After the third or fourth time seeing her struggle with her beloved pet, I crossed the street to help. Up close, you could easily tell she was a grown woman.

I asked if she wanted me to walk her dog for her, offering up my leash for hers. She bowed slightly with a big smile and accepted the much thinner, red leash, gladly relinquishing her inch-thick blue rope.

Linda was a tiny thing. Quite pretty, too. Her dark, no-nonsense haircut curled softly behind her ears, brushing the tops of her shoulders. She wore a blue shirt with yellow flowers along the trim, and straight pants, cinched tight around her hips. Not fashionable to most, but it suited her.

We traded leashes and traded the idle chit-chat of two strangers. Linda was thirty-one and had moved to Alabama a few years before. When I asked about her dog, her face brightened. She told me all about Cassie, her golden retriever, so I told her all about my chow, Chi. We laughed about how we both rushed home after work to let our dogs out, joking that we prioritized our fur babies' needs above our own.

"What do you do for work?" I asked.

"I'm finishing up my oncology fellowship at UAB.[2]"

Fellowship? Oncology? At my puzzled expression, she said, "I'm a doctor. I'll be a practicing *cancer* doctor in a few years."

Whoa. "You look so young to be a doctor!" I said. She nodded, speaking quickly. She was obviously wickedly intelligent. Far more intelligent than me. And yet, oddly, refreshingly humble. It became clear through her constant questioning that she'd much rather hear about me than talk about herself.

Naturally, I obliged by answering her quick questions, but I tried to squeeze in a few of my own. I had planned to impress her by explaining what I did for work, but being the executive director of the NASA-affiliated Challenger Learning Center seemed less remarkable now. She wasn't much interested in the program anyway. She had more questions about the months I'd spent working with Royal Caribbean Cruise Line as the Ship Youth Director (and eighth in command, I had pointed out).

"Were you ever afraid of drowning?!" she asked, her eyes wide. I shook my head, laughing that of all the things I had just shared, the possibility of drowning *on a cruise ship* was what she couldn't get past.

As we approached my apartment, I thought of casual ways to invite her inside that wouldn't be too forward. Offer a cup of coffee? It was evening now, so maybe wine would be better.

"You don't have to walk me all the way," she said, giving me an I-can-take-care-of-myself smile. "I'll take her from here."

I grabbed Chi's leash, then gestured to the building closest to us. "This is my apartment."

---

[2] University of Alabama at Birmingham

"Oh. That's mine." She pointed to the building a few doors down. She looked at the blue leash still in my hand. "Well. Thank you," she said, grabbing the leash. The moment it was back in her hand, the dog yanked her forward, sensing they were close to home. "Good–night–Kermit," she said between tugs.

Well, maybe tomorrow, I thought. Hopefully, she'd be out at the same time. I waved, watching her disappear into her apartment without giving a second glance in my direction. Her door promptly shut. I breathed a laugh, urging my chow, so light by comparison, into my apartment.

What a perplexing woman. Dainty exterior. Formidable interior.

The next evening, in a sense of déjà vu, I saw her in the same spot across the street as the hot Alabama sun cast a long shadow across my small furry companion. I looked down the street before jogging over, putting an easy smile on my face, and offered her my leash without a word. She gave me hers with the same huff of relief as the day before, and smiled back, showing her teeth. One tooth stuck farther out than the rest. I smiled wider, falling in step beside her. She wore straight, uptight pants that hung from her like a curtain on a rod. And she looked gorgeous. She seemed more relaxed today. Her walk less hurried, her shoulders less hunched.

We talked about everything we could think of. Family, food, more about our dogs, our favorite movies ... our conversation just flowed. The silence between topics, which I would have otherwise felt compelled to fill, felt strangely natural. When the sun eventually fell below the tree line, an orange glow suffused the air. Her skin looked smooth, almost golden, in the warm light. *Damn, she is beautiful.* She caught my eye and smiled, before taking Cassie's leash and returning home.

The third day, I waited for her in the same spot. As she approached, I took Cassie's leash. Before she took her third step, she launched into a discussion, as if the twenty-four-hour period since I'd last seen her had been but a momentary interruption of our conversation. She filled me in on the latest news at her work. I nodded along. *I could listen to her talk for hours,* I thought as I smiled to myself, enjoying the warmth of the sun as well as the conversation.

By the time we made it back to our apartments, she stopped and turned to me. "I have an extra ticket to see *Rent* this weekend. It's a Broadway musical," she said, a slight bounce in her step. "Would you like to see it with me?"

She was asking me on a date. *She* was asking *me* on a date. I debated whether I should tell her I'd seen *Rent* five times already. I decided against it. "Yeah, I think I can do that."

She beamed, showing her crooked little tooth that I was becoming increasingly fond of, then waved goodbye.

"Goodnight," I said, already counting down the hours until I'd see her again.

My façade didn't last long. I'll never forget her face as I lip-synced every number of *Rent*, unashamed of my little ruse. She looked at me with some mixture of frustration and what I'd like to think was admiration. After the show, she told me I wasn't the only one keeping secrets. There had never been an extra ticket, she told me. She wanted to be sure I would go before buying it. I gaped at her, exaggerating my shock, though I felt unusually flattered. On the way to the car, I thought of where I could take her out again the next night. I eventually landed on Milo's, my favorite local burger joint. Who doesn't love burgers?

The following night, as I walked us to a table near the back, I turned to Linda. "These are the best burgers in town. They're a staple of the community!" I said, gesturing to the grand establishment around us. She eyed the greasy picnic-style table with less than enthusiasm and sat down across from me. A fly buzzed close to her ear, and she shooed it away, scrunching her eyebrows.

Once we ordered our food, I knew she'd be won over. Milo's wasn't known for fancy inventions stuffed with blue cheese or swapping lettuce for spinach; they were known for the best classic burger around. Linda absently shooed another fly from her face and asked, "So why are you so giddy to take a girl on a date to a hole-in-the-wall place with trash food?"

I sputtered. I admired her honesty, albeit brutal honesty. However, I was prepared to stand by my decision. I shared their standards for quality ingredients, customer service, cleanliness (I cringed a bit at that last one, but it was summertime, when every restaurant has flies). She didn't seem convinced, though she ate the burger without complaint.[3] I coughed, preparing to steer the conversation away from my lack of good judgment in food establishments. "So. What made you choose UAB?"

"UAB called first," she said, then took a bite of her burger. I stared at her, waiting for more. She finished chewing, then told me she had two options to choose between for completing her fellowship: Vanderbilt in Tennessee, her first choice, and UAB. When UAB called to offer her a spot in their program, she thought it better to have a spot than none at all, so she accepted. Then Vanderbilt called the next day. She imitated the phone call in a higher-pitched voice, "Linda Lee, it's so nice to speak with you. We are excited to offer you a position to complete your fellowship in our Vanderbilt program..." to which she responded, "You called a day late." The Vanderbilt woman tried to politely persuade Linda that there was no harm in changing one's mind, but Linda wouldn't budge. "I've already given my word to UAB, so I'm going to UAB," she replied sincerely, albeit begrudgingly, then hung up the phone. I stared at her, my jaw slack behind closed lips. *Add loyalty to the list,* I thought, shaking my head. She smiled innocently, completely unaware of what that look was doing to my insides. *Thank goodness UAB called first.*

The next evening, I invited her to my apartment to cook her dinner. I made some semi-impressive dish involving salmon and potatoes, then served us both a glass of red wine. I'd spent all that morning cleaning up the dirty clothes next to the couch and the pile of dishes in the sink. I considered myself cleaner than your average single guy, but even I couldn't tell you the last time my socks made it into the hamper.

After giving her a short tour, I said I'd like to see her place sometime. "No, it's not clean," she said, taking a sip of her wine, then abruptly changed the subject. Odd, but I wasn't going to push it. *Maybe she's dirtier than me,* I thought. That wouldn't have been the first surprising thing about this woman.

Weeks later, I found out that she was *not* dirtier than me. When I stepped into her apartment for the first time, I realized why she'd delayed. Cassie, that poor, sweet, innocent dog, was treating everything like a chew toy. She

---

[3] She later told me her friends couldn't believe I had taken her to Milo's for a second date. I just laughed. To this day, I stand by my decision.

had even *eaten through* the bathroom wall. I was stunned into silence, then managed, "Linda, what the hell is that?"

She covered her face, groaning, "It's where I have to put her when I go to work. It's embarrassing, I know."

"*Embarrassing?* She's been eating drywall and two-by-fours to get out of there!" A piece of drywall broke off in my hand as I inspected the hole in the wall. "Linda," I said, dusting off my hands, "you should have named your dog Cassie *Cujo*."

A few days after the Cassie Cujo incident, I called Linda to confirm our next date. "Sorry Kermit, I have to cancel." *Damn.* I mentally ran through the last conversation we'd had. It was inside her apartment, I'd said something about her work ... had I said something to offend her? I thought things were going well... I waited on the other end of the line, imagining a number of outlandish reasons she'd be canceling our date. Yet not once did I even consider it had something to do with a basketball game.

She told me the North Carolina Tar Heels team had made it to the next round of March Madness, and she was not going to miss it. "Kermit, it's a priority," she told me over the phone without a hint of remorse. I laughed, picturing Linda in an oversized basketball jersey.

"You're telling me, basketball is so important to you, that you're willing to cancel our date? *And* you're beautiful. *And* you're a doctor?!" I couldn't believe it. "Are you trying to turn me on right now?"

Silence. "Yeah, well, don't get too turned on by it," she said, flatly.

I was grinning ear to ear, strangely enjoying the fact that I was annoying her with my questions. "So, you want to watch it together?"

Another short pause. "No. I need to focus." Focus? During a televised basketball game? Could this woman get any more perplexing?

Eventually, after some pleading and begging, Linda allowed me to watch the game with her. Not five minutes in, I found out what she meant by "focus." She was an absolute animal. Close to halftime, she was stalking around the room, waving her arms, yelling... her face bright red. I'm not saying I was ducking behind the couch as she flung cushions across the room, but I did move the coffee table out of the way, fearing for my beer every time she jumped to her feet from the couch to scream a curse word at the coach or referee.

It was both terrifying and entertaining. Downright funny too, watching her coach every play as if it made any difference. And no matter what, she was never happy with the score. If UNC was up, there was too much time left on the clock; if they were down, she'd swear under her breath until they made a good play, cheer, then go back to swearing. She kept looking at me, if I were judging her crazy passion and devotion to the game. She couldn't have been more wrong.

Watching this five-foot tall Asian woman pacing the floor was downright puzzling. It was like watching Dr. Jekyll turn into Mr. Hyde: when we passed another dog on the street, no matter how sickly or pathetic, she turned into a pink-nosed puddling mess on the pavement, petting, patting, scratching, cooing. Put that same googly-eyed puppy lover in front of a basketball game, she turned feral. She was the strangest, most awe-inspiring and intimidating thing I'd ever seen.

Our days started to blend together. I eventually stopped asking and just knew she'd be coming over for dinner, and we fell into a comfortable routine. Trade leashes, walk the dogs, eat dinner, drink wine, cuddle on the couch.

One evening, I'd made a steak dinner with grilled vegetables and was waiting for her "mmm" of approval. I had known her preference for meat by now, and this knowledge was reinforced after she'd helped herself to seconds while the vegetables sat barely touched on her plate.

I was in the middle of talking about what to cook next, ribs maybe, when Linda interrupted me, "Well, I don't cook. So..." Silence. Then, awkward silence. Her eyes locked with mine. *Am I supposed to say something? She's looking at me like I'm supposed to say something.*

"OK," I said. She smiled at that, then kept eating. *Well, I guess I better learn how to cook more variety,* I said to myself.

That evening, wine glasses sitting mostly empty on the coffee table, Linda said, "Alright, it's time for me to go." This exit had become part of our routine. Each night, she'd lean over, give me a brief kiss, then let herself out the door. I'd say goodbye, she'd walk the forty-five steps to her apartment, then I'd lean my back against the closed door and think, *How on earth is someone like her interested in me?*

A few months later, I finally gathered up the courage to tell Linda how I felt. I wasn't ready for the I-love-you moment, but knew I needed to express my feelings about the growth in our relationship. We'd yet to have any serious conversations about our future together. In previous relationships, there had been an unspoken expectation that I was supposed to make the first move. To be the man, the person to decide where the relationship was going. But with Linda, everything felt different. It was easy, natural. I'd told her things I'd never told anyone before. I was so comfortable with how things were going, I hadn't thought it important to discuss the future.

Her head rested comfortably in my lap and her eyes were closed. A small smile spread on her lips as I stroked the hair back from her face over and over again. She was beautiful. Her soft skin, her slender arms. Even her crooked smile, despite how much she hated it. She had hit my arm the first time I called her "my little snaggle-tooth." The name stuck after that.

"I want to tell you something," I said. She sat up, and I grabbed her hand, pulling her towards me. *Here goes,* I thought. My life was about to shift. I was finally going to tell this invulnerable, maddeningly introverted yet brilliant woman my feelings. "I'm emotionally attached to you," I said, smiling down at her.

She was looking at me, smiling. And then, she wasn't. She slowly withdrew her hand from mine. "What?"

"I'm emotionally attached to you," I repeated, stupidly mistaking the look on her face for confusion. "I feel really good about this."

By this point, her face more resembled something that would normally have suggested that I'd just killed her dog right in front of her. I'd said something wrong; I just didn't know what. So, I waited.

19

She stared back at me. "That's it?"

The air felt too hot, and my palms abnormally sweaty. The wine suddenly tasted bitter. "Well, uh, yeah." I said, reaching for her hand. "I–I don't know what else you want from me right now."

Well, the conversation declined further from there. Despite all the relationships I'd been in, despite all the women I thought I understood, I realized I knew nothing. Not a damn thing.

One day later, while Linda was at work, I executed an idea. I'd been brainstorming ways I could make up for the night which resulted in Linda calling friends to ask, "What does 'emotionally attached' even mean?"

Using an old camera I had in my apartment, I took Cassie down to the park and captured shots of her running and playing in the grass. It was a true glamor-shot session. I felt so professional. After snapping close to one hundred photos, I decided on the best one to frame as a gift for Linda. Then I made sure Cassie was back in the apartment before she got home.

The next night, I gave Linda the wrapped gift with the frame inside. She looked surprised, then suddenly smiled wide, tearing the wrapping paper. It was a black and white photo of Cassie sniffing the air in Rushton Park near a concrete statue we often visited on our walks. Linda stared down at the frame. "You took a picture of my dog?"

"Yeah, I did!" I said, feeling proud of my secret project. I prepared myself for an onslaught of kisses and a "Thank you, thank you, thank you!" leading up to the final, "How'd you pull this off?" I watched her face, waiting for a smile. A giggle. A flinch.

"Well… it's nice… but why did you choose black and white?" she asked. Her nose crinkled like some food critic who'd just tried the soup of the day and was not impressed. "And you came into my apartment without me there and took Cassie? You kidnapped my dog?"

I swallowed, trying not to show my disappointment. I put a smile on and stared at the frame still half wrapped in the now crinkled blue paper. "OK," I managed to say, then returned to the kitchen to finish dinner. I drank the rest of my wine in one swig, thinking. *Clearly, I have more work to do, but I'm battle-tested now. Come hell or highwater, I will succeed with this woman.*

Over the next several months, I knew I had met my match. We were like two gladiators with different fighting styles—respectful of the opposing warrior, and both utterly convinced each was tougher than the other. But I knew she was tougher. She could outwork me at every point.

When I finally told her I loved her, I asked, "Do you know why the Roman Empire wasn't built in one day?"

"No."

"Because a woman wasn't in charge."

Maybe I already knew this, but Linda had convinced me that a woman had the ability to accomplish so many more tasks and be so much more multifaceted than a man.

It wasn't long after I told her I loved her that I knew I wanted to spend the rest of my life with Linda. But I was still young, still naïve and completely clueless on how to woo the woman I was dating. When I zigged, she zagged. I simply couldn't keep up with her brain or her energy. I couldn't escape the thought in the back of my mind telling me that Linda could do better than me.

We'd been dating for nine months, and I still hadn't met her parents. She'd already introduced me to her godparents, Tom and Vicki, the couple who'd taken her under their wing, and supported the immigrant teenager adjusting to American life. They'd supported her transition from high school to college, and all through her residency, even after Linda and their son had broken up (more on that later).

Now it was time to meet her real parents. We packed overnight bags and drove to Raleigh, North Carolina, and arrived at their apartment complex around noon. We made it ten feet from the car before the smell of sour vinegar and fish assaulted our noses. I turned to Linda, confirming with a wide-eyed expression that her olfactory experience was the same as mine. She laughed, then nodded toward the house encouragingly. The smell only got stronger as we entered. Once my eyes had stopped watering, I managed to take a breath without tasting fish. I, a southern boy from Alabama, was having a cultural existential moment. Linda explained it was kimchi, a traditional Korean dish.

In Korean culture, if one wants to be perceived as a basic cook, they must first know how to make good kimchi. Made up of salted cabbage, coated in a paste of garlic, ginger, onion, fish sauce, fermented shrimp, and chili powder, the concoction is left to ferment in an onggi,[4] for days or months on end. The stuff never spoils.[5] Before refrigerators, the onggi was buried to prevent freezing in the winter and keep cool in the summer. Once fermented, the result is a bright red, sweet and sour mixture of vegetables, softened cabbage, and spices. A staple in any traditional Korean household.

When she had first asked me to meet her parents, I had asked what they were like. She'd said they were like any Korean parents: shy, somewhat intimidated by American men—especially ones over six feet tall, she'd told me, chuckling—but her parents hadn't expected much else from someone like her. "Someone like you? You mean, a badass that is going to lead her own life with no influence from others?" I'd asked. She'd laughed, her cheeks turning a shade darker.

When Linda had first moved to America, she had considered education as her path to freedom, to financial independence. She could take care of her parents in their old age, and could find a husband when *she* was ready, not when it was deemed appropriate for her age. Growing up in South Korea, she'd observed an imbalance between men and women. If a man got tired of holding his briefcase, he would drop it behind him and know, without having to look back, his wife would pick it up and carry it for him. In more traditional households, if a man needed to use the restroom in the middle of the night, his wife was expected to get up and warm the seat for him. Even for her sons. I'd told Linda this custom seemed inhumane, but she'd shrugged, saying it just wasn't the life she wanted.

---

[4] A handmade Korean clay pot traditionally used for storing kimchi and other fermented foodstuffs.
[5] In culinary slang, we say "ferment for infinity and beyond."

I had considered what her parents would think, seeing me walk through the door, a whole foot taller than her father, but she'd assured me they knew all about me, so I shouldn't be nervous. I still was. On the drive, I'd mastered two Korean words: "gamsahabnida," meaning "thank you," and "annyeonghaseyo," meaning "hello." Perhaps they wouldn't sustain long conversations, but they could at least start one.

I followed through the door after Linda and smiled at her parents. "Annyeonghaseyo," I said, bowing slightly as Linda did the same. She grinned at me, pleased.

Their English was of a similar capacity to my Korean, and a sense of relief washed through me. Our first conversations consisted of crude sign language, with the occasional conversation between Linda and her parents. The evening was mostly silent, but a quaint kind of silence. Like the kind found in a library.

The following morning, Linda woke early to shower, leaving me to explore the house. Ilho stood in the living room, clad in a tattered white wifebeater (which Linda later told me was his go-to look) and baggy khaki shorts. He smiled when he saw me. "Annyeonghaseyo," I nodded, smiling back. I tried not to stare at his partially exposed left breast.

He nodded toward the kitchen. "Help you-self." I looked behind me, confused. He said again, "Help you-self. Help you-self." He was gesturing to the pot on the stove. From the stench, or to some, *aroma*, I assumed it was a pot of boiling fish. I looked over the edge and the skeleton had separated from the flesh. I inhaled a shallow breath, trying not to wrinkle my nose at the pungency, and got an equally strong whiff of more kimchi. I waved as politely as I could, dismissing the offer. "Very fragrant, but that is a little heavy for breakfast at 6 a.m.," I said. "No, thank you."

He laughed, understanding. Then, with a twinkle in his eye, he shuffled over to the freezer and pulled out a T-bone steak. The frozen steak hit my hands with a smack. "Kermit, help you-self," only it was more like, K-O-U-M-I-T with no distinct "r" sound.

I looked down at the steak, now freezing my hands, then back up at his sincere smile. I gave an awkward laugh, glancing toward our bedroom where Linda was bound to be getting out of the shower soon. I willed Linda to walk out and save me from disappointing her father in offering me what I assume he thought was "American food."

"Koumit, help you-self, help you-self."

I shook my head, trying to put the steak back in the freezer. *Linda, you better be getting out of that shower soon.* My hands were now painfully frozen. This exchange went on for another five minutes before Linda finally came out of the bathroom. I gave her a look somewhere between amusement and "Save me!" as Ilho retrieved a frying pan. She looked between me, the now thawing chunk of meat in my hands, and her father. Then, something like a bark left Linda's lips, telling him to leave me alone. I'd yet to hear her yell anything in Korean and hoped to God I'd never be on the receiving end of it. I gave her a silent "thank you" and put the meat back in the freezer, making fists to return the feeling back to my palms and fingers.

To my relief, we spent the rest of the morning doing what any normal family does when welcoming someone to the family – looking at photo albums. Linda's mom, Okja, pulled out scrapbooks of Linda as a baby, and as a toddler wearing adorable dresses and overalls. We laughed together, despite not understanding each other more than "thank you" and "hello."

As we got up to leave, Linda held onto her mother for a long while. Okja's health had continued to decline since moving from South Korea. She stood four-foot-nine on a good day, and was always cold, dressed in at least three layers of clothing with a scarf, even in the summertime. On the drive home, Linda told me she wished her mom could live closer, believing the warmer weather would be good for her.

I finally asked Linda why her father would shove a frozen T-bone steak in my hand at 5:30 in the morning. She laughed, telling me that unlike American meals, Korean food isn't split into food groups based on times of day. Korean families eat kimchi with practically every meal. If you could eat something for dinner, you might as well eat it for breakfast and lunch, too. My stomach turned just a bit.

I'm no Anthony Bourdain, but I like to think I had a reasonably sophisticated palette after spending my early twenties sailing to destinations around the world. To this day, there's nothing on this earth that ever came close to kimchi,

The following day, we were back in my apartment. Our wine glasses sat empty on the coffee table next to the nearly empty bottle of wine. Linda sat with her legs crossed over mine, her cheeks more pink than usual from the extra glass she normally refused.

Sitting in our usual spot on my couch, we laughed, recalling the sight of her father in shorts and a wife beater. I told her I could still smell the kimchi as if it were being held under my nose. Some crooner song was playing on the radio, and I sang the words out, enjoying the warmth of her so close to me.

She looked at me, then, eyes huge and dark and lovely. "I want to have your baby," she blurted out.

I blinked as my jaw hung open, not even trying to hide the shock on my face. *What did she say?* Her hand jumped to cover her mouth, eyes widening even more. Her cheeks were flushed, and she looked away quickly.

That can't be what she said. It was so "un-Linda." *That can't be what she said.* I replayed her outburst in my head over and over again, letting it fill my head like the buzz from my wine. Only much better. Then, I seized her bright red face and kissed her once. Then, I kissed her for a long time.

I took Linda's not-so-subtle hint. She was a few months shy of needing to choose a practice, and other than my attempt at confessing my "emotional attachment," we'd kept all talk of the future pretty brief. But this was different. She wanted to have *my baby*. I started running through all the things that had to happen *before* a baby came into the picture.

The next day, I called her *god*parents to ask for her hand in marriage. I asked them for the same reason I met her godparents *before* I met her real parents. They were in some senses the ones that looked after her.

When Linda was seventeen, she met Tom and Vicki Hunt. Their son Chris, who was fifteen and a sophomore, sat in Linda's same biology class. One day, Chris came home complaining that he'd lost the top score to "some girl who didn't even speak very good English." A few weeks later, he asked that girl to the Dixie Classic Fair. Weeks later, after meeting Linda's family, Chris asked Linda to be his girlfriend. From what I've gathered, their relationship always looked more like study partners who enjoyed the competition of trying to outscore each other.

In school, Linda was determined to succeed. Much in the same way she learned English, she wouldn't quit until she became the best. If her high school had nerds, Linda was a nerd. Tom joked that only after two years of speaking English, Linda could have taught the class better than the high school English teacher (and he was probably right).

Linda came over to the Hunt's house most days of the week and enjoyed the company of Tom and Vicki just as much as Chris's. Their fat golden retriever, Muffin, became Linda's best friend, while their cat, Ginger, hated her as much as she hated Ginger. (I can't say for sure, but I'd bet money Ginger was the reason my wife became a dog person.)

Dr. Thomas H. Hunt was an interventional radiology doctor, and Vicki was a charge nurse (among other things) who specialized in movement disorders research. Both earned their medical degrees from Wake Forest School of Medicine (which later prompted Linda to do the same). Tom had a knack for telling great stories, and always kept dog treats in the ashtray of his car or in his pockets on neighborhood walks because, "well . . . you just never know when you're going to meet a new friend." Though his six-foot five stature could fill any room, his wife Vicki would argue his warm heart and positivity were even larger. Vicki treated Linda as her own; she took Linda shopping for new clothes and taught her everything she could about the western world. Through vacations, shopping trips, and frequent family dinners, Linda became the daughter they never had.

When Chris asked Linda to the junior prom, neither she nor her parents could afford a prom dress, so Vicki asked all the neighbors if any of their daughters had an extra dress she could borrow. She received nearly a dozen loaners. On the big night, she chose a light pink satin dress with a bow on the shoulder and wore a string of pearls around her neck. Vicki told her she looked beautiful before snapping a photo of her sitting on their couch.[6]

---

[6] Thank you, Vicki Hunt, for this beautiful picture of seventeen-year-old Linda.

Chris and Linda stayed together through their second year of medical school before they broke things off. (To this day, I don't know why she ended things with Chris; I never asked. All I know was that their breakup allowed her to someday choose me, and I'm not about to question a miracle like that.)

When I first met Tom and Vicki, Linda swore there was nothing to worry about, but all that was running through my mind was, "Why on earth was this brilliant doctor, who grew up among *other* brilliant doctors, who even dated someone who later *became* a brilliant doctor…dating me?" I had nothing to bring to the table. No degrees or specialties (not unless you count my excellent sense of humor). I wasn't scholarly in the slightest sense of the word, and yet, Tom and Vicki loved me because I loved Linda. For them, that said more about me than any piece of paper ever could.

Prior to 2014, scientists and deep-sea divers were baffled by strangely symmetrical circles etched into the sand on the ocean floor. These intricate underwater works of art, decorated with seashells, sand dollars, and coral were a mystery, until they discovered the mating habits of the white-spotted pufferfish. When the male pufferfish is trying to find a mate, he will spend days on end crafting an extraordinary geometric design, in hopes that just one female will find his creation worthy of her attention. But these male pufferfish don't just make it once. They work tirelessly, swimming back and forth, carving the sand with their body to prevent the current from sweeping it away. His art must first be seen, and it must be perfect. He's so proud of his own creation. He struts like John Travolta in Times Square with "Staying Alive" playing in the background, attention getting like the king of pop, Michael Jackson, dances like Kevin Bacon at the end of *Footloose*, and like Patrick Swayze in *Dirty Dancing*, trying to steal the show to win over the girl he loves. Their romantic pursuit is relentless.

Why do I bring this up? Well... I am a male, white-spotted pufferfish. A touch flashy. A bit extra. Like Apollo Creed being lowered to fight the Russian in the boxing ring, I overcompensate with self-generating positive mojo, perhaps to hide my flaws. In the pufferfish philosophy, if anything is worth doing, it's worth overdoing. Though my flair fell woefully flat with my little snaggletooth on most occasions, my over-eager capacity to gain her attention never ceased.

When I proposed to Linda, it was on the beach. Using a total of thirty tiki-torches, I made a forty-foot circle just off the shoreline of the Gulf of Mexico. In the center, I had written a note and tied it to a rock: "Dig where the stone lies." Linda spotted the thirty lit torches from a distance and stopped, rolling her eyes at me in a way that convinced me I'd made the right decision. She knew exactly what was happening when she approached this gargantuan display. She told me she wanted to be surprised. She told me she wanted it to be subtle. But that just wasn't my style. She read the note, dug up the glass bottle, and read another hand-written note that was inside the bottle:

"I'm going to show up for you every day. This is my promise to you. Will you marry me?"

I got down on one knee as she turned around, and I held out my hand for hers. She was smiling. I was smiling, too. And, for some unfathomable reason I have yet to understand, and have yet to thank God enough for, she said yes.

Note from Kermit: *Are you dying to see what these pufferfish can do? Scan the QR code below. You'll be glad you did. [**Editors:** Kermit, it's just you who's into this. You're literally being a pufferfish RIGHT NOW.].*

CHAPTER 2

"Find a Way to Keep Dr. Farmer"

A few weeks after getting engaged, Linda was given an opportunity to interview at a large practice in Atlanta. It was her first real offer, and despite her initial wish to go back to North Carolina to be closer to family, she was considering it.

"Oh honey, you don't want to do that," I told her, shaking my head. "Really, you don't want to do that." I could think of nothing worse than sitting in bumper-to-bumper traffic on a Thursday afternoon for three hours.

"Why?" She looked up at me from the pamphlet with "15 Things To Do in Georgia" held in her hand. She gave me a confused frown. "I think it might be a good thing."

Once Linda had set her mind on something, it was next to impossible to change it. I paused, reviewing my next words carefully. If there was one thing Linda couldn't deny, it was logic. No arguments needed. "OK, but I'm gonna go with you," I said, then told her to schedule the interview for, I don't know, say, four o'clock next Thursday.

Linda ran the numbers. In Birmingham, Alabama, we were two hours from downtown Atlanta. Linda, being Linda, decided to leave four and a half hours before the interview. And right on cue, we hit dead-stop traffic five minutes into Georgia. I swear, Atlanta was gobbling up Georgia like the Borg of Star Trek, just eating everything in its path. I could hear a string of curse words beneath her breath as she careened her head back and forth, attempting to pinpoint exactly what was causing the holdup. "It'll be fine, Linda," I said, squeezing her hand. "I'll bet it'll clear up in less than fifteen minutes."

31

An hour later, due to construction delays and one wreck, we had made little progress. I hid my smile as Linda's face became an increasingly dark shade of red. Finally, after another hour of honks, cut-offs, and fighting with GPS, we parked in the parking lot a full ten minutes before the start of the interview. "I am over this!" she said as we got out of the car together. Linda looked like she was two honks shy of decking the next person she saw in the face. She gave me a curt nod, hurriedly running her hands through her hair and brushing invisible dust from her pantsuit. I smiled, giving her two thumbs up as she disappeared behind the door with the woman carrying a clipboard.

My plan was complete.

Someday, when I meet the Almighty, and he asks me why I was thankful that my dear fiancé's first interview to be an oncologist was sabotaged, I will say, "Because I am a sick bastard who would rather listen to his wife curse all the drive to Atlanta and back in one day, than have her sit in hours of traffic every morning and afternoon for the rest of our lives." Linda didn't much consider the impact of such things on our quality of life, so I took this responsibility upon myself. I wish I could have taken all the credit, but Atlanta's congested, four-lane highway sabotaged Linda's mood so efficiently, I didn't even have to conjure up supporting arguments. Her decision was made before she even stepped into the building.

Days after the Atlanta fiasco, Linda received an invitation to visit a conglomerate private practice in east Alabama. Having never been to Auburn, I held no bias towards their traffic patterns, and therefore, made no attempt to sabotage the interview.

We arrived a day early to check out the town. After exploring the city, we pulled over to the nearest building, a massive Methodist Church. The senior pastor was walking on the sidewalk and introduced himself as Dr. George Mathison. He recommended we visit the Amsterdam Café, a place known for their unique menu with a flair. We thanked him, promising we'd be back to attend the service that following Sunday.[7]

We were at a table on the patio, seated underneath a thick cover of trees, watching cars drive by on a college campus we knew nothing about. Linda took a bite of some portobello mushroom concoction, then turned to me and

---

[7] And we did for the first three months, though we thought their contemporary service was not quite contemporary enough for us.

said, "I could do this." The town reminded Linda of Chapel Hill, the home of North Carolina University and her beloved Dean Dome, the renowned basketball stadium. I nodded and said I could do this, too. The next day, after a successful interview, Linda strongly considered the position. After speaking with many mentors and considering and even praying about it, she accepted.

In the six months prior to moving, we built our home in Auburn. Linda was in her last days of fellowship, and we were neck-deep in wedding planning. Linda didn't want anything too elaborate, and despite my desire to pufferfish my way to the front page of the local news, I believe the wedding day belongs to the bride. So, I put away my ideas and stuck to a traditional-style wedding. Mostly. Early on, I suggested to Linda that instead of having a traditional cake topper, we should find someone to make a custom topper with my male chow and her female golden retriever. "Like a little version of us, but our dogs," I told her excitedly. She said no, cringing at the corniness of it. So, tuxedo man and white dress lady it was.[8]

We were married on May 25, 2001, at the Vestavia Hills United Methodist Church, in a suburb of Birmingham. Like all weddings, there was celebration, joyful memories, and *lots* of laughter. I cried at the altar before, during, and after the ceremony. With her inescapably cerebral mind, she kept asking me, "Why are you crying?" I just wanted to scream, "BECAUSE I LOVE YOU WOMAN!"

We were so different, but perfectly matched for each other. Walking out of the church in front of our families, all I kept thinking was *She chose me. ME!*

It was Springtime in 2002 by the time we settled into our new home. Linda started at the clinic right away and quickly discovered the pressure of bearing the title of "doctor." During her residency, all through her fellowship, there was always someone above Linda to have the final say, take the responsibility, step in when overwhelmed. Not now. Linda was in her own practice; she had the final say. Her fellow oncologist had been the only other oncologist in the community for several years, and naturally, Linda felt rather alone. Like

---

[8] She later regretted this decision, and for the first time, and maybe the only time, the words "Kermit, you were right," escaped her lips. It's a moment I'll never forget.

anyone thrust into that kind of authority, in life and death situations no less, it terrified her. She wondered if her training and talents were good enough.

Our first several weeks went by in a blur. Linda was hardly at the house. And when she was, it was to fall asleep on the couch after delivering a twenty-minute recap of her day. In less than a month, our once peaceful routine of walking dogs, drinking wine, and snuggling on the couch was no longer the norm. A new chapter had begun.

I had known our life was going to change, especially for Linda, but for the first time, I caught a glimpse of my future as the husband of an oncologist. But I hadn't the slightest idea how to be a husband, let alone a husband to a *doctor*. I constantly questioned how I could best support her. Give her a back rub? No, she'd just think I was looking for what comes *after* the back rub. Make her dinner? Well, I've been doing that for over a year already so it wouldn't make much of a difference. Do I leave her alone? Offer to help in some way?

When I said "I do" at the altar, my own path was permanently changed. Not irrelevant, but secondary. I had known this from the beginning once Linda told me the kind of doctor she was going to be. But living it out was its own challenge.

Growing up with a traditional male-dominant viewpoint, I always pictured walking through the door to the fragrance of my wife's freshly cooked dinner and being greeted by hugs and kisses from her and the children. Instead, when my wife comes home exhausted from the day, I am the one who greets her at the door with a kiss and says, "Welcome home, honey." I was the support. The manager of the home.

This reverse dynamic caused me more issues than Linda; though, luckily, neither of us were inherent fighters. We always remained respectful of each other. When we occasionally wouldn't agree, it usually ended with me conceding and Linda silently accepting her victory. She didn't gloat, but I took her soft smile as some indication I was doing something right.

I suspect God knew Linda needed someone who wasn't going to fight back. When you take a woman with that much vinegar, and pair it with someone equally acidic, you're left with even more bitterness. But pair that vinegar with some oil, things just might turn out OK.

On days when Linda would come home, either frustrated with herself or with the situation of one of her patients, I learned the most important thing I could do was sit down, shut up, and listen. It wasn't always easy, but after I learned the beatings would continue until I kept my mouth closed" I stopped interjecting.

Six months into her practice, Linda had established herself as the "compassionate doctor" among her patients. She and I recovered some semblance of a routine, even allowing ourselves to enjoy cuddling on the couch again and drinking wine. Or rather, I was the one drinking wine. A few weeks after getting married, Linda confessed she never liked red wine. She only drank it because she didn't want to tell me she didn't like it. I gaped, asking her if she'd been drinking red wine for over two years all because she didn't want to hurt my feelings. Her slow nod only made me feel worse, though we laughed about it later.

But then, almost overnight, Linda's number of patients tripled . . . and soon quadrupled. The other oncologist in the practice had a family emergency and was now on medical leave for six months. Linda told me the news with a slight shake in her voice but kept her chin high with that beautiful smile on her face as she walked out the door to meet her new patients. She was now the only general oncologist in all of eastern Alabama.

Many specialty doctors take a maximum of twelve to eighteen patients in a day; Linda saw an average of twenty-four, sometimes twenty-six. On a good day, she ran an hour behind. On the average day, two. On a harder day, three. Her patients never complained. They knew, despite the pressure to get in and get out of an appointment, Linda would never rush through a visit. This was the hallmark of her craft. She provided as much information as she could in as much time as was necessary. Her time belonged to no one but her and her patients. As long as she sat on that stool in front of a patient, they had her full attention.

On average, doctors work four days out of the week, alternating with another doctor to have some semblance of work-life balance. Linda didn't have another doctor to allow that balance, so she worked five days. Every decision. Every diagnosis. Every treatment plan. Every pep-talk. It all rested on her shoulders with no other doctor to consult. And she bore it beautifully (not to mention my badass woman was only seven months out of her fellowship).

Witnessing Linda wake up in the morning was a marvel, though tragic at the same time. What started at 5:30 a.m. transitioned to 4:30 a.m. then settled at 3:45 a.m. Within three seconds, the alarm clock was slapped into silence, and within eight seconds, she'd be in the shower. I didn't know the workload of other doctors, but all I could think was, *She's a Marine. She accomplishes more by 9 a.m. than most people do all day.*

Up until that point, I hadn't thought there was much else I could admire about Linda. Of course, I was wrong. Every day was a full day of visiting with current patients, overseeing chemotherapy, and interpreting blood work to ensure the right drug dosage and treatment were being administered. On top of all that, she rounded the hospital daily, sometimes twice, and visited new patients.

For each visit, she had one ultimate goal: prevent the patient from asking "What do I do now?" Before leaving any patient, she'd lay out, step-by-step, what they could expect, in the short term and long term. Most patients only retain a fraction of what's said to them, so she gave extra time to answer their questions, and when they inevitably had more, she answered those, too.

For new patients receiving initial diagnoses, Linda reserved forty-five minutes. She wasn't going to rush through delivering a diagnosis, no matter how optimistic she was. After explaining the kind of cancer they had and what treatment she'd recommend, she gave the remaining twenty to thirty-five minutes to the patient. Some were spent in tears or in prayer, others in silence, others filled with questions. And somehow, she always knew what her patients needed. She knew which patients needed kindness and which needed candor. She knew when they needed encouragement or compassion or when they needed a good ass-kicking. And they knew she would never stop fighting for them. When a lean, healthy, thirty-five-year-old woman got diagnosed with breast cancer and was convinced it was a death sentence, Linda looked her unblinkingly in the eye, grabbed her hand, and told her she needed to fight: "Your attitude will kill you before this cancer will. Your family can't do it for you. I can't do it for you. Only you can make this decision to live."

Getting someone to choose life, especially when they don't want to own up to the responsibility, is hard, but Linda wouldn't let them do otherwise. On some occasions, with particularly stubborn patients, she'd say, "Let me tell you about the patient on the other side of this wall." It was always the same thing: "Someone with statistically worse cancer than you is fighting and even beating the odds because of their attitude." Cancer is a war against the body and mind; Linda didn't just tackle the physical disease; she fought the emotional fight alongside the patient as well.

When a twenty-seven-year-old got diagnosed with cervical cancer, and her husband left her, saying "it isn't what he signed up for," Linda wrapped her arm around her shaking shoulders, and with tears in her eyes, said, "You can still fight this. I will be with you every step of the way. You have a family here. I'll be here."

Though I love to refer to my wife as Wonder Woman, she couldn't supernaturally heal her patients, or control the outcome of their disease. She relied on something greater, more powerful, than herself. Each morning before speeding out the door, she'd spend time in prayer. Reading the Bible, preparing for the day, asking Someone else to work through her. Every time she held a patient's hand, she knew it wasn't just Linda holding their hand, nor was it just her words guiding them, or her prayer comforting them. It was the strength she asked for every morning.

When a patient doubted their ability to beat their cancer, Dr. Farmer would click-clack her little heels down that hallway at five in the morning just to give them a proper ass-whooping and dose of encouragement. When another patient going through chemo dreaded losing their hair, Dr. Farmer was there to sympathize and listen without judgment. Most importantly, Linda stood for quality of life. Sometimes, it would be a patient's time to *stop* fighting. When the body gave up before their mind, she would tell them, with equal earnestness, that it was their time to rest.

She was vulnerable and authentic. She allowed herself to feel the pain of others, witnessing their sorrow, their regret. And instead of building a wall of defense, as normal humans are prone to do, she opened herself to them fully. She did so every day without complaint (she even shared with me this sacred gift, showing me how to share openly with others without fear[9]). Once her eleven to fifteen-hour day of seeing patients was over, she'd come home only to evaluate herself. Not to me, or even out loud, but to herself. Constantly asking if she did all she could for her patients. Then, not by

---

[9] Without her desire for authenticity, I'd have never been able to write this book.

choice, she'd collapse onto the couch, fall asleep, get woken up by me to come to bed, then wake up at 3:45 a.m. the next morning to do it all over again.

One evening, I asked her why she insisted on waking up five hours before seeing her first patient. Or why she bent over backwards to fit in more patients and to see all of them for as long as she did. (In America, the average oncologist spends sixteen minutes or less with each patient during scheduled visits.[10] This of course isn't entirely the fault of the doctors themselves; hospitals often give quotas in the same manner as traffic policemen: "See X patients by the end of the day.")

She answered me in the form of parables, using examples of what her patients were going through. She told me about a grandmother whose pain medication got stolen by her grandson and how that patient would need some accommodation and as much comfort as possible when the pharmacy refused to fill the prescription early. She said it was because of the terrified little eleven-year-old boy sitting beside his grandfather, who was dying, and how that boy would need time to process, to cry, or to ask questions. Then she said it was because of the twenty-eight-year-old pregnant woman who needed chemotherapy at fourteen weeks and was terrified to lose the baby; that mother would need more direction, more reassurance, and more kindness than anyone else. "Kermit, when a patient looks at you and asks, 'If this were your grandmother or baby…' I can't brush off a question like that. What I tell them impacts how they view their futures."

I didn't say anything. I couldn't. So, I just nodded, knowing I could never fully understand the burden she carried.

Somehow, despite the stress of oncology, she fell in love with its complexity. It's what first drew her to it. The nuance of each case was like a rush for her. How a patient's genealogy, body mass index, age, muscle mass, and a thousand other factors created a challenge so unique, only a handful of individuals would attempt to solve that puzzle. She was a part of that handful. To her, finding the path forward was like playing a three-dimensional "chess" board from *Star Trek*.[11] Impossibly complex, seemingly improbable to understand, and yet, she learned.

---

[10] Markman, Maurie. "Oncologists Spend Too Little Time with Patients, Too Much on EHR." Medscape, April 26, 2018. https://www.medscape.com/viewarticle/895319#?form=fpf.
[11] Remember … nerd^2

I was awed, inspired, and completely baffled by it.

For the six months when Linda's partner was on leave, we'd both go to work, then come home, then eat dinner, then fall asleep. Not an ideal environment for newlywed intimacy, either physical or emotional, but real life set in. Fast. We found a routine that worked, and I chose to make the best of the hard times, particularly the ones that frustrated Linda the most.

Though Linda named herself after Wonder Woman, she was no Amazon. Her 109-pound, two-by-four-shaped, sixteen-year-old physique didn't scream *authority*. When meeting new patients, she'd make the first impression in the same manner: warm smile, firm handshake, some laughter, then get down to business. She'd start the conversation with, "Tell me how you are today," then reassure the patient by telling them, "I will be here with you through this journey." Then, as if reading from a cue card being held up behind Linda's head, they'd respond: "No thanks, I'll just wait for the doctor to come in." (There's probably only one thing that could make my wife madder than these words, and that's if anyone referred to or called her an "oriental." To this, she'd snap back, "I am not a rug."[12])

After this initial, typical, thirty-second encounter, she'd take a deep breath through her nose, point to the black rectangular name tag on her white lab coat that read, "Dr. Lee Farmer," and say, "I *am* your doctor."

She'd then come home in a huff because some six-foot burly man insulted her stature, and she'd want sympathy from me. And I'd give it, though I couldn't help but laugh a bit to myself. She was just so cute when flustered.

By this point in our marriage, I assumed I had gotten past my inability to woo my wife. She did marry me after all. So, when Linda arrived home at 7:13 p.m. one evening, she walked through the door, hung up her coat, bent down to remove her shoes, then stopped halfway down. She saw me sitting on the rug by the fireplace with one leg propped up. I had a skewer in one hand and an elaborate fondue tower set up with running melted cheese in front of me.

---

[12] My father made that mistake just once after meeting Linda for the first time. She was such a badass!

"Hi honey!" I said, beaming. She looked from me to the fire, then back at me and sighed. "Oh, good heavens, not fondue by the fireplace *again*." Then with a huff of exasperation, she unloaded her things onto the kitchen island. I gawked at her. What the hell kind of woman says, "Not fondue by the fireplace *again*"?! *I'm trying to do something special, something romantic here! I can't win here, woman.*

Though my ego was dampened for a while, I couldn't blame her. It hadn't been my first attempt at a romantic gesture, and those were usually met with equal scrutiny. I began to realize she wasn't ungrateful, or even moody from dealing with other people's problems all day. She was just inherently different than I am. One night, when we went out with some friends, the topic of "love bombs" came up in conversation, defined as excessive attention, or an outpouring of affection on someone. Then, my wife, so lovingly, so endearingly said, "Kermit is less of a love bomb and more of a love *tsunami*. It just comes out of nowhere and hits you!"

We all burst into laughter while Linda just sat there, earnest as ever. Between giggles and irrepressible snorts, I realized how true that statement was. My love for Linda *was* like a tsunami. Uncontrollable. Powerful. All-consuming. I sat there smiling like an idiot at the "compliment" while Linda glared at us, having meant it to be a true comparison: a catastrophic event that left casualties in its wake. She eventually laughed too, not realizing that she'd just permanently trademarked my affection for her. Between giggles and irrepressible snorts, I realized how true that statement was. My love for Linda *was* like a tsunami. Uncontrollable. Powerful. All-consuming.

My love tsunamis only escalated over time. I couldn't help that the woman I chose to marry was single-handedly the most fun person to annoy. When you take an introverted, servant-minded, type-A personality, and have them come home to a serial self-deprecating jokester, what could anyone expect? I couldn't help that the woman I chose to marry was single-handedly the most fun person to annoy. My schemes mostly ended in laughter, though on several occasions, they were followed by scoldings or eyerolls.[13]

On our wedding day, we said vows like any other couple ... "I vow to love and cherish you from this day forth, until ..." but I also made a second vow.

---

[13] Those could have been trademarked, too.

A vow I said to myself every day, even on the days I didn't want to. I vowed that while she would serve the many, I would serve her. I would serve the one even if it meant I never got served. I vowed that would be enough for me. But it wasn't until our twelfth year of marriage that I understood just how blind I had been. One night, an epiphany like a fluorescent lightbulb went off in my head, and I interrupted Linda during one of our couch conversations, "Wait, are you saying that every time I do something nice for you, you feel like you have to do something nice for me?"

"Well yeah. So just stop doing it so I don't have to do anything for you."

"Linda, that's terrible. I don't want you to feel like every time I do something for you, you feel burdened, or pressured to do something for me." Memories of all the over-the-top, and in my own estimation, undeniably crazy things I'd done for her over the course of our relationship started playing in my mind. All the backrubs. Every time I surprised her with a gift. That one time I spent two months uploading all of her CDs onto an iPod, all for her to say that she wouldn't ever use an iPod and preferred her CDs. All this time, I'd thought I was showing her how much I loved her. "Linda, you have to know that's not why I do anything for you. Paybacks aren't needed on a team."

She scoffed, throwing up her hands. "Kermit, are you going all Dr. Phil on me again?"

Despite the sting of my wife thinking my motives were, more or less, conniving, I eventually found comfort in this newfound truth. Finally, after years of hunting, exploring, and failing to decode this fortified woman, I'd cracked a piece of the puzzle.

On our wedding day, we said vows like any other couple ... "I vow to love and cherish you from this day forth, until ..." but I also made a second vow. A vow I said to myself every day, even on the days I didn't want to. I vowed that while she would serve the many, I would serve her. I would serve the one even if it meant I never got served. I vowed that would be enough for me.

When Linda's partner returned to the practice, a lot had changed. In her absence, the patients once under the care of the senior doctor had become close to Dr. Farmer, and naturally, some preferred Linda's care. When going through chemotherapy sessions, counseling, grief, and any other step of the cancer journey, patients are bound to connect with their current, present doctor; Linda was that doctor for every patient in eastern Alabama for some time. So, when it came time to re-balance the patient distribution, many patients had strong opinions. Some chose to stay with Linda, others grumbled, for weeks, over being transferred. Patients complained—to the nurses and anyone they could find. They wrote emails. Made phone calls. It brought tension that Linda couldn't ignore, no matter her efforts.

The medical practice Linda worked in had many other subspecialties, and treated Linda like a singular cog in the wheel. To protect all involved, I will not expand on what happened next. Suffice it to say this: The practice and Dr. Farmer went their separate ways. Soon after, late one evening, with Linda assuming her regular position with her head in my lap, looking up at me with glassy, red eyes, she said, "I think it's time to move back to North Carolina." She shared her fear over the thought of leaving her patients. She knew no one would love her patients in the same way she would. But even she couldn't deny how exhausted she looked. Eyes red and puffy. Smile more strained than usual.

Before making a decision, we let ourselves daydream of what our future could be like. She pictured herself teaching in front of the classroom at Bowman Gray Center for Medical Education at Wake Forest University, educating the next generation with all she'd learned, all she'd grown to love. I imagined the conversations we'd have over dinner, the dates we'd go on after she'd get out of teaching classes at the university, the peace we'd feel being closer to family. And for the first time in three months, I saw some of the light return to her eyes. We couldn't think of any downside. So, we decided to move back to North Carolina.

During this time, the CEO of the local hospital called my cell phone. We spoke of our plans to leave for North Carolina. He let me finish, then spoke of the community needing Dr. Farmer. He wanted to see if she would consider coming on staff at the hospital, which was across the street from the clinic she had left. Linda rounded there daily and had a very positive rapport with the staff. I didn't know until later that the head of the hospital board, a man named E. L. Spencer, had said, "I don't care what you have to do. Find a way to keep Dr. Farmer."

I couldn't blame them.

That's exactly what I'd been telling myself since the day I'd met her.

CHAPTER 3
A Closet, an Oath, and Moral Injury

*P*icture a fork in the road. The path on the left is long and winding, thick with mist and branches strewn across the road; the one on the right is short, with a clear view of the end. This is the way of cancer. There are two paths for every cancer patient: You either hear, "You *can* fight this," or "You *cannot* fight this." You can't choose which road is yours; that choice is made for you (some say by God, others say by the evil of the world, still others by chance). Both are equally hard roads to travel. One might think those who are told they *can't* fight receive the harsher sentence. It's bleak. It's final. However, it is often brief. Those who are told they *can* fight are in it for the long haul—pain is stretched further, emotions are worn thinner, and the "what ifs" hanging in the air constantly make it hard to breathe. But regardless of your path, there's a doctor walking alongside you. This walk forms a bond unlike any other. Through hours of exhaustion and countless tears, your oncologist willingly guides you down your path. Taking your hand, telling you jokes, wiping your tears, whispering prayers, offering encouraging words. Then finally, when you reach the end of the road, be it the short, clear path, or the long, winding one, they hug you close and say, "I'm so proud of you."

Linda had walked down both roads with countless patients thousands of times since living in Auburn, and she was prepared to do it thousands more.

Linda and I would be staying in Auburn.

Linda accepted the full-time subspecialty position at the hospital as the first-ever oncologist to practice in the hospital. Her patients told her how ecstatic

45

and relieved they were to hear she wasn't leaving town. They also shared how desperately they wanted to remain in her care. But Linda was no longer an employee of the doctor-owned practice across the street. She was employed by the hospital, and to "steal" patients was, to put it lightly, frowned upon. And while she didn't encourage it, half her patients requested to transfer to her care when Linda's clinic at the hospital was up and running.

At the hospital, it was all hands on-deck to figure out how to set up an oncology practice on short notice. Aside from Linda's desire to stay with her patients, the hospital's ability to handle the everyday issues (infrastructure, billing, etc.) that sealed the deal for Linda, who, while many things, was not an entrepreneur. When the hospital first pitched the idea of building out an oncology practice within its four walls, all she said was, "I just want to see patients, that's it," and like everything else she ever said, she meant it. She had no desire to be "the boss." In negotiations, we made sure they understood their role, and more importantly, *her* role; Linda would see patients, the hospital would run everything else.

But intention is often less practical than reality. Linda was, once again, the only oncologist in the practice, and all the weight that had been lifted by the return of her partner at Internal Medicine Associates, settled back on Linda like an unwanted familiar blanket: long days, on-call, non-stop patients. Linda was running on five to six hours of sleep a night.

Over the next few months, the hospital had to find enough physical space to "fit" Linda's practice. Their solution was to use the Human Resources or HR offices.

Picture walking into a hospital. Lobby in the front, seating area off to the side somewhere, elevators towards the back. Now picture a typical cancer clinic: it's about the size of a doctor's office with enough space for a waiting area and small lobby, and several rooms designated for doctor visits and infusions. So, if you can imagine trying to squeeze a bulldog into a breadbox, that's about the same challenge they had trying to fit Linda's new clinic inside the hospital's old HR offices.

My wife could handle more stress than most, but to say it was a blessing from God when LeAnn Cox walked through the door would be an understatement. LeAnn was hired to be Linda's receptionist and was her first employee. With a bubbly attitude and sweet Alabama drawl, she greeted every patient with a wide, welcoming smile. LeAnn's desk sat in the first of four rooms; the clinic in its entirety was about the size of four bathrooms put together. LeAnn often joked she could high-five each patient in the waiting area without ever having to leave her desk. Each room fit one desk and one rolling chair, and just enough space for one person to pass in between. For infusions, they used an old conference room across the lobby, which had Linda running back and forth between patients every thirty minutes to an hour. "If I give 100 percent, Linda gives 400 percent," LeAnn joked with the patients. "I swear, that woman has eighty tabs open at all times." It wasn't far from the truth. When Linda would go on what I called her "apology tour," explaining to each patient exactly why she was running two or three hours behind schedule, she never had to look at the charts or wonder who her next patient was. It was as if she memorized the schedule and could speak to each person's medical and personal history, like a file permanently stored in her brain. It was a marvel.

As with any new operation, particularly one squeezed into a sort of closet, there were hiccups with paperwork, retrieving patient info, and long wait times, but her patients never bothered voicing complaints. If the lack of space and paper charts weren't enough explanation, they told LeAnn they knew Linda was doing everything she could to make sure they were taken care of. As the number of Linda's patients increased, another receptionist was hired to help fill in the gaps.

Linda showed up at 5:30 a.m. every morning, early enough to see her other patients, so that by the time the rest of her staff arrived, she wouldn't skip a beat. Not a minute went to waste in her schedule. She moved like a whirlwind without breaking a sweat.

When watching Linda move at such a neck-breaking pace, it's easy to assume she did so easily. But even if the work is *extremely hard,* and it was, Linda's love for her patients is what made it "easy." She never had to put on a smile or fake a laugh. She didn't pretend to be bright and cheerful; she just was. She knew her patients' pain and understood that to make them feel heard and loved, there was no time for complaints, hiccups, or "bad days." Every day, according to Linda, was a good day. But what was easy for Linda, was not so easy for me. When the person you love gives every ounce of their energy, every day, to the point where there's mere ounces left, it's hard to just sit by and watch. Her patients never saw what I saw: the pure exhaustion that practically glued Linda to our couch when she was home. As she would nod off after a long day, I'd receive vigorous hand waves and sharp "I can handle myself" attitudes when trying to help her get to our bed. Even dead-tired, she insisted on walking herself. It was her way of saying, "I got this."

Within eighteen months, Linda's practice grew beyond the closet and was moved to a larger space. Though still smaller than what most oncology practices need, the new space did have a proper infusion room. Further, more nurses joined, which helped distribute the workload.

But within the same wisdom as Uncle Ben in *Spiderman,* with more space comes more responsibility. And Linda felt that responsibility. When someone's mind is tasked with one thing, twenty-four hours a day, seven days a week, they're bound to wind up in one of two categories: insane or exhausted. The only reason my wife didn't end up in the former category is because she found some local doctors to take her on-call shifts. She paid them handsomely, and it allowed her to "relax" two days a week.

To understand Linda, I think of the book, "Men Are Like Waffles, Women Are Like Spaghetti," by Bill and Pam Farrell. Unlike male doctors who typically have an easier time compartmentalizing, Linda's thoughts flowed together like spaghetti; even when she was off, meaning not on-call, she would still check the obituary the second she woke up in the morning to see which of her patients had passed overnight. Even when sitting on the couch in her best attempt to unwind, she'd feel tense, knowing the phone could ring any minute. Whether she was on-call or not didn't matter.

Most days, I tried to understand her spaghetti mind. It was less of an obsession, more of a compulsion. I couldn't blame her for not being able to compartmentalize; it wasn't how her brain worked. On other days, I simply wished for her to find a sense of peace. A space away from everything related to cancer.

Finally, Linda was able to recruit another oncologist to join the hospital. Having a singular point of failure in her practice was a disaster waiting to happen: If anything happened to her, the clinic would come to a screeching halt. So, she recruited Brandon. who allowed Linda—for the first time in three years—to have some time for herself.

"Ya know, honey, with all this *free time*," I teased, "you could finally find a hobby." My use of the term "free time" always raised my wife's hackles, making it all the more fun for me. However, for anyone *not* in the habit of receiving eyerolls and glares, I wouldn't recommend calling the days when a doctor is finally off, "free time."

When a doctor is finally not on-call, visiting patients, or otherwise at the mercy of their practice, they're typically asleep, or at least too exhausted to do much else. But again, we're talking about a superhero.

"Well, Andrea *did* just invite me to do a half-marathon with her," she said, unphased by the jest.

"Um, running isn't exactly the hobby I had in mind." I had selfishly pictured her choosing something we could do together. Like gardening. If that woman had suddenly grown a green thumb, I'd have the pots and soil delivered by morning.

But of course, Linda happened: "After she invited me, at first, I thought, *That's crazy. I could never run a half-marathon.* But then, I started asking myself, *Well, why couldn't I?* Not to mention, with how often I tell my patients how important their physical health is, I shouldn't be the exception."

Of course it related back to her patients. How could I have expected anything else? I took a swig of my beer. "If you say so."

"I was also thinking you could do it with me."

I choked.

The beer burned my nose as I coughed. "Honey. That sounds great. But . . . I think I'll just meet you at the finish line. With my beer." I gave her a cheers and took another swig.

"Fine," she said, laughing. "But I think I'm going to do it."

So, a few months later, that's what she did. In preparation, she'd run every evening after work, whether it was pouring rain or over one hundred degrees. Nothing could persuade her otherwise, not even me. She had found a new obsession that was great for her mind.

On the rainy days, I'd try to convince her to stay inside. Secretly, I wanted to cuddle and watch a movie, or reenact my classic "fondue by the fire," but my offers were never accepted. Her retort was always something like, "If I don't allow my patients to make excuses, why should I use rain as one?"

Relentless, stubborn woman. But even I had to admire her dedication. And frankly, over time, I saw that it benefited her ability to practice. When she wasn't running with friends from work, she'd run by herself, using the time to de-stress. I was happy for her, despite having hoped she'd find a way to de-stress *without* exhausting her body.

Within a few months, she started booking half-marathon trips, then trips to other cities for full marathons. Running became a permanent piece of the Linda puzzle. A passionate oncologist, a dog enthusiast, a basketball fanatic, and now, *a runner.* I couldn't have been prouder, standing at the finish lines with a beer.[14]

Every marathon, she received a medal. A few years in, and our top dresser drawer was full of them, all tangled up together. "Honey, we need to hang those up," I said one day. after seeing her add another to the pile. "You know, display them with some pride." I had the perfect spot in our mudroom all picked out. I just needed to convince the boss.

---

[14] Just kidding. I tried it, but my beer was confiscated at the entrance. Apparently, those sorts of enjoyments aren't allowed at marathons.

She shrugged off the idea (of course) saying she didn't care one way or the other. If there was one thing she hated, it was acknowledging her own accomplishments. The next day, I went online, searching for the right medal display rack. I finally found one that made her smile. Along the top, it read, "DO OR DO NOT, THERE IS NO TRY." Standing next to it was Yoda, one of my wife's favorite philosophers. From then on, Linda hung up each new medal, smiling as she did so. I'd actually done it. For once, I'd given Linda a near-perfect gift.

She was never the fastest runner, and she never tried to be. For once in her life, she didn't care to be the best; she was just comfortable doing *her* best. Still, strangely, even after years of running, I could never tell if she truly *enjoyed* it, or if she only did it for her patients. *That's so Linda.*

Before Linda became an oncologist, she knew she had a duty to fulfill to her patients: learn as much as possible, then share as much as possible with your patients. To her, it was part of the Hippocratic Oath she'd taken:

"My all that I hold highest, I promise my patients competence, integrity, candor, personal commitment to their best interest, compassion, and absolute discretion, and confidentiality within the law.

I shall do by my patients as I would be done by; shall obtain consultation whenever I or they desire; shall include them to the extent they wish in all important decisions; and shall minimize suffering whenever a cure cannot be obtained, understanding that a dignified death is an important goal in everyone's life.

I shall try to establish a friendly relationship with my patients and shall accept each one in a nonjudgmental manner, appreciating the validity and worth of different value systems and according to each person a full measure of human dignity.

I shall charge only for my professional services and shall not profit financially in any other way as a result of the advice and care I render my patients.

I shall provide advice and encouragement for my patients in their efforts to sustain their own health.

51

I shall work with my profession to improve the quality of medical care and to improve the public health, but I shall not let any lesser public or professional consideration interfere with my primary commitment to provide the best and most appropriate care available to each of my patients.

To the extent that I live by these precepts, I shall be a worthy physician."

The Hippocratic Oath was written by Hippocrates, known as the Father of Medicine, around 400 B.C. It was created for physicians who were dedicated to the advancement of medicine through science, rather than through superstition and religion. Though this oath is no longer mandatory in our modern world, my wife lived and practiced by this principle. To her, it was second only to Someone else's book.

When you place that devoted, hyper-driven, Hippocratic-Oath-following oncologist in the modern world of cancer medicine, where you're expected to churn out patients every fifteen to twenty minutes, what do you get? Either a doctor who decides to sacrifice their commitment to the Oath (which is more common), or a doctor who doesn't care about the rules of engagement, and instead will do everything they can to provide the best care for their patient. Take a wild guess which category Linda fell into.

Me, being a mere mortal, couldn't fathom what it was like to handle this kind of burden, so Linda explained it to me like this: pick your favorite book or movie, then try to explain it to someone in less than seven words.

Take *Harry Potter* for example. Do you try to summarize the plot of all seven books? Should you explain the dynamic of good and evil, the magic of Hogwarts? Should you talk about the underlying message of friendship and loyalty? It feels impossible to even try, and yet, this was what Linda dealt with, every day, with every patient. Not only was she trying to share over a decade's worth of education and research, but she needed to communicate with empathy, kindness, and candor (that was more of a Linda requirement, rather than a Hippocratic one). And on top of all that, the information that needed to be shared changed depending on the status of that patient. She'd take their age, mental attitude, weight, overall health status, and a number of other factors before deciding which information was vital. But that's the thing about oncology. When one's life is hanging in the balance, all information becomes vital. So how do you choose what to share?

Linda refused to make that choice. Her oath was more important than some hospital quota determined by someone who wasn't face-to-face with a suffering or dying patient. When she was allotted twenty minutes, she would spend forty-five, or even sixty. Then, on to the next, with the same patience.

Few other doctors understood Linda's patience, but Dr. Wes Gleason was the exception. Wes was a radiation oncologist who had a thriving private practice in the hospital before Linda. Over the years, they became close friends and colleagues; they understood each other in a way unique to doctors who face death on a daily basis.

If my wife was the yin, Wes was the yang. In some ways, he was the complete opposite of Linda. As I liked to tease, he was "born to be mild," so docile that he made Linda look down-right ferocious. If a patient was rambling on or talking in circles, Linda would listen to the patient, then address their immediate concerns. Wes, on the other hand, would let the patient prattle on about every fear, even the ones he'd already addressed, then patiently answer them all again without batting an eye.

Over the years, I became increasingly thankful for Wes and his friendship with Linda. He gave her someone to laugh with on stressful days. He cared about patients the same way my wife did. But above everything else, he understood the burden of fulfilling their Oath under the restrictions of the modern, Western healthcare system. He knew, just as well as she did, it was a battle they'd have to fight every day: serve patients with patience, while responding to ever-increasing pressure to "meet quota." But, even with each other's companionship, they were both struggling mentally and physically.

Many may try to describe what Wes and Linda were feeling as "burnout," a term first coined in the 1970s as a "toxic combination of physical and emotional exhaustion, feelings of cynicism and detachment, and a diminished sense of personal and professional accomplishment."[15] But to use such a commonplace word would undermine the true challenges Linda and Wes, and many other Oath-abiding medical professionals, face every day.

---

[15] https://www.cancertherapyadvisor.com/home/news/taming-the-flames-of-burnout-in-oncology/ Talia Fioretti, "Taming the Flames of Burnout in Oncology," Cancer Therapy Advisor, December 1, 2023, https://www.cancertherapyadvisor.com/home/news/taming-the-flames-of-burnout-in-oncology/.

There's an ancient cautionary tale called "The Parable of the River." It begins with a village beside a river; one day, one of the villagers sees a baby floating down the river. Naturally, the villager scoops the baby up and brings it back to the village. The next day, two babies are seen floating down the river, so two villagers save those children. Each day, more and more babies continue to float down the river, and more villagers come out to save the babies, until one day, there are more babies than villagers. And yet, the babies continue to come down the river. Finally, the village becomes overrun. Everyone is exhausted and frustrated they can't save every child. Feeling hopeless, one villager suggests they walk up the river to find the reason so many are coming down the river in the first place. Surely, if there was a way to prevent the babies from falling in the river, then they would all be saved, and their village could continue to thrive. But the elders of the village scold the outspoken villager.

"If you were to trek up the river, imagine how many babies would be lost in your absence!"

Our current healthcare system, with its quotas and demands, can force doctors to focus on "triage" care: providing the best possible care in the least amount of time to solve the immediate problems with an influx of patents that need to be seen. But this does not always equate to the best possible care overall. What if our doctors had more time? Would better decisions be made? I think Wes and Linda would respond, "certainly." Generally, our present system simply doesn't allow the amount of time it takes to provide *the absolute best care possible*. Instead, doctors' schedules are limited by the overwhelming demands of our healthcare system, and doctors find themselves making decisions on how to provide the best care *within the constraints of the time offered*. So, many doctors live each working day wondering if, given more time, could they have provided better care?

Some doctors shrug this feeling off. Others, such as Wes and Linda, internalize this burden, experiencing what's called "moral injury." And such mental and emotional injury is catastrophic in the field of modern medicine, because, ultimately, this type of injury attacks the only people who can truly save the "babies" at all. Moral injury attacks the "villagers" themselves knowing you could do more and provide better care with more time. I suggest in modern medicine we can do better with the patient journey by using modern tools. More on this later.

In Wes's life, I saw the effects of moral injury first-hand. For over twenty years, Wes's soul was pushed and pulled in every direction by his patients, for whom he cared (almost) as much as Linda. His heart and responsibilities were stretched too thin, at home, at work, and even in his church. On November 25th, 2011, Wes committed suicide, leaving behind his wife and three boys. His death came as a shock to everyone, and it was one of the only times I ever saw my wife cry.

When you give everything and it's still not enough, what do you do? *That* is moral injury. It's debilitating, and it's a problem worth solving. I'll go on the record by saying C-Suite leadership in hospitals can do better in this area. They need to see the warning signs and treat the frontlines to ensure their medical staffs are safe and provided for as they are the ones pulling us all from the water. The future of practicing healthy medicine depends upon this.

CHAPTER 4

Hurry Up and Wait

*W*hen I was twenty-two years old, I was offered a human child for five U.S. dollars. In my early twenties, I had been on contract with Royal Caribbean Cruise Line. Between our monthslong contracts, we had six weeks to travel or just enjoy time away from work. I typically chose *not* to return home, but instead, showed up at the airport, passport in hand, and picked the cheapest flight where I thought an adventure awaited. Silly? Maybe. but I was in my twenties; ergo, my only thought was, *What's the worst that could happen?*

The cheapest option on one particular trip was Thailand. Once I flew into Bangkok, I headed north by train for the jungle region thinking, "This seems fun." When I got off the train, a man approached me, asking if I wanted to buy an elephant. *Of course I wanted to buy an elephant.*

They used the term "buy" rather loosely. It more accurately meant "rent." Once you bought your elephant, you'd ride it up to where you wanted to go, then sell it back.

With my tour guide and two other tourists, I started my two-day trek to a remote village in the northern tip of Chiang Mai. If you're picturing a path of dirt and some road signs, think again. Imagine something closer to *The Jungle Book*. All I could do was trust that my guide knew where we were headed as our elephants' thunderous, clumsy feet left all vegetation flattened in their wake.

Whenever the guide spoke, I noticed his teeth. They were the color of licorice, stained by his use of what they called "betel nut." Betel nut is a mild hallucinogen found in the local Areca tree and has a thousand-year-history of usage, at least. Supposedly, it prevents tooth decay and smelly breath, though I can say for sure that it produces effects more aptly associated with chewing tobacco.

After a two-day hike, we reached a small village. Bamboo huts with thatched roofs were scattered between the trees. A handful of women were selling their hand-made jewelry, while groups of men crafted rafts from bamboo. When a raft was complete, they'd ride it down the river to sell to those who lived in the village at the bottom of the river. Each raft sold for about six U.S. dollars. Once sold, they'd make the trek back up to the village to start crafting their next raft. The entire process took ten days. For all that work, they made six dollars. In ten days.

For two nights, I slept under the protection of a mosquito net. During the day, I was fascinated by the villager's slower pace of life. When a raft was finished, rather than take as many rafts as they could, they'd simply ride the one that was complete and float down the river. I couldn't help but contrast the American work-model that relies on efficiency and speed, to the care these women put into each handmade item.

On my third day, a woman came up to my porch, yelling the same words over and over again. "1,800 baht! 1,800 baht!" I looked around confused, unsure if she was talking to me. As I looked down, I saw in this woman's outstretched arms an infant, wrapped in a bundle of dirty cloth. The local villagers had begun forcefully pulling her away, but it didn't stop her from crying out, "*1,800 baht! 1,800 baht!*" I stared at her, dumbfounded. That amount, 1,800, baht was the equivalent of five U.S. dollars. Was this woman trying to sell her own child?

Once the woman had been shooed away, the villagers returned to their daily duties as if nothing out of the ordinary had happened. During that day I watched mothers take a draw from a heroin cigarette then breathe the fumes into their infant's mouths with a kiss. I learned this was a normal practice, used to stop them from crying. Infants and adults alike had withdrawals from the drug, but the smoke helped both in the moment.

That afternoon, we climbed up our elephants and made our way back to a local town. Throughout our trek, the woman's anguished face kept coming back to me. When I closed my eyes, I saw that baby: it's too-small body, wrapped up in that stained, dirt-covered cloth. I could still feel her distress. See the sweat shining on her forehead, on her neck. It made me feel sick.

For weeks, I couldn't shake the cloud of disbelief and sadness that hung around me. I was disgusted by what she did. Staring at me, screaming "1,800 baht!" How could she have valued the life of her child so little?

At last, over time, my nights became quiet again. I was no longer stirred by that experience. Then about six months later, a woman holding an infant to her chest reminded me of her, and I was back in that moment. I could picture what my life would have looked like, living in that village. Making six dollars a day, trying to keep my infant, not even healthy, but just alive. Then the truth struck me, and I felt sick all over again. Those tears hadn't been shed by a cruel mother. They weren't even shed for herself. It was for the baby. There wasn't a lack of love for her child, but an abundance of it. The kind of sacrificial love that allows you to do the unthinkable for the sake of your child's survival. Some women go into prostitution to keep a roof over their children's heads, or parents forgo their own meals so their children can continue to grow. Teenage mothers give their babies up for adoption, because of lack of finances.

I saw myself through that woman's eyes. Some six-foot-something, broad-shouldered, physically capable white male, who ostensibly had the means to give her child a better life, wherever he came from. Even if it meant giving up what meant the most to her, she wasn't going to be selfish.

I've carried the weight of that child's life with me until this day. From the moment I realized his mother's sacrifice, I knew I was going to adopt a child.

Back when Linda and I were dating, a few months shy of getting engaged, we were walking in Rushton Park. It was clear our relationship was getting more serious, so I finally felt brave enough to tell her about this experience. I didn't know where this would take the conversation, but it was extremely important to me. I ended with, "Because of this, I've always wanted to adopt."

Linda stopped, then squeezed my hand in hers. She looked up at me, the widest smile on her face. "*I've* always wanted to adopt!"

I huffed a laugh. *I hadn't been expecting that,* I thought, pulling her to me. I wrapped my arms around her as she leaned comfortably against my shoulder. I felt a sudden peace wash over me, over us both, as we stood there, wordlessly holding one another, envisioning what our life was going to look like in a whole new light.

I knew God's hand was over us that day. I couldn't have told you how or why Linda's and my relationship worked, or why in the world she chose someone like me, but one thing I did know was that the journey we were on was the right one.

It's 2006, six years after that conversation in Rushton Park. Linda's clinic inside the hospital is booming. Between fifteen-hour days and Linda still religiously waking up at an ungodly hour every morning, life felt as busy as it ever had. One night, Linda got home around 6:30 p.m., which was early for her. It gave us a chance to relax for a bit longer before she inevitably fell asleep. We sat for a while, enjoying the silence of being together. When jobs consist of endless updates, explanations, and conversation, sometimes *not* talking was our best way to reconnect.

"I think we should have a baby," she said, shocking me out of the silence.

Well, that was unexpected. "Um, you kinda got a lot going on, woman. Things are a bit much right now," I said, beginning to weigh that possibility against our current reality. The idea of my wife moving a mile a minute while carrying a bowling ball strapped to her belly, all while click-clacking from one patient's room to the next, just didn't seem feasible. But the last thing I wanted to do was shut down her idea. I knew the desire to have a baby, even in the midst of intense, daily duties, was a plight shared by many female doctors and nurses. We sat quietly for several minutes, my last words hanging heavy in the air. "What about adopting our first child instead of having one first?" I said. "It's a longer process, which will give us time to prepare. And maybe, once we know what it's like to have one, we can talk about having our own?"

Her expression was inquisitive. I could see the wheels turning. She knew I had a point. "OK," she said.

Well, that was easier than I'd expected. Normally I'd be met with arguments, or some form of push-back. But she said OK. So…OK. Now I just needed to figure out how the heck anyone started the process of adopting a child. It was a new task for me, but not so unlike many of the others Linda had asked of me over the years.

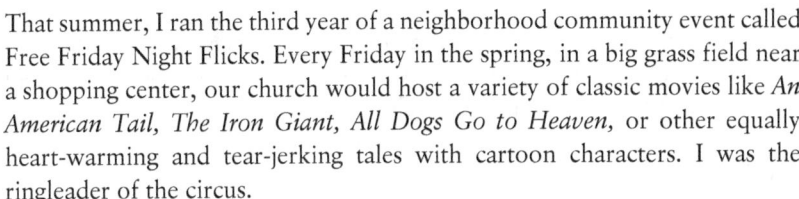

That summer, I ran the third year of a neighborhood community event called Free Friday Night Flicks. Every Friday in the spring, in a big grass field near a shopping center, our church would host a variety of classic movies like *An American Tail, The Iron Giant, All Dogs Go to Heaven,* or other equally heart-warming and tear-jerking tales with cartoon characters. I was the ringleader of the circus.

One Friday evening just before sunset, *The Iron Giant* was about to start playing when I got an email sent to my Blackberry.[16] It was the single most precious thing I had seen in my entire life: a picture of "K2006 – 862," or so the little piece of paper read just below the child's tiny feet. I was looking at a picture of our son. He was so small that he could have fit in the palm of my hand. Perhaps it was a sign, or we just got lucky, but he was wearing a onesie the same shade as Carolina Blue.[17] I immediately called Linda. "Check your email!"

We sighed together, looking at this perfect Korean child. Just like that, it was decided. Linda had to return to work, but she promised we would grab dinner to celebrate. After hanging up the phone, I hit "reply" to the email:

"Yes, we want him."

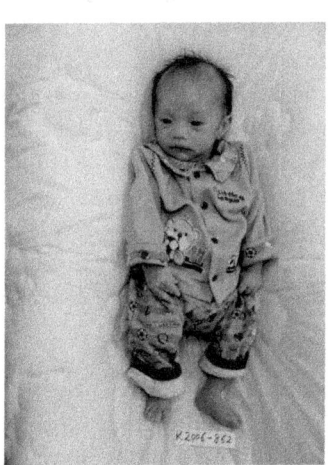

---

[16] May she rest in peace. A moment of silence for the greatest phone ever invented.
[17] The popular and official color of the University of North Carolina,

We spent the evening basking in our newfound parenthood. "What should his name be?" I asked, looking at the photo for probably the thirtieth time.

"How about 'Spencer'?" she said, taking a bite of her sandwich. That was fast. I waited for some explanation or meaning behind her choice. She kept chewing, as if the answer should have been obvious to me.

"Spencer? Why Spencer?"

She shrugged. "Well, I'm only here because of E. L. Spencer, right?"

Maybe not the name I would have chosen, but at the time, I was just excited to know we could stop searching. "Alright. Spencer." We leaned in close, looking at the tiny screen of my Blackberry. With tear-filled eyes, we held each other's hands and prayed for our new son, Spencer.

Then came the waiting. With no end date for when we could go to South Korea to bring Spencer home, each month felt longer than the last. It eventually started to catch up with me.

Now, I love grocery shopping. I *love* it. It's where the community is, it's where I strike up conversations with my people. But let this serve as my formal apology to my community, particularly all the mothers who frequented my local grocery store that Fall and Winter. You know that strange feeling when you're out in public and suddenly you feel someone staring at you? Like a prickle on the back of your neck? Or when you catch someone's eye and look away, but you still feel them staring at you? That was me, doing the staring. Every time I'd see chubby little legs sticking out the front of a grocery cart and watch their eyes track across their new and foreign landscape, all I could think was how that picture would include me: one day soon, I'd be holding Spencer's tiny hand as we walked through the grocery store together.

When a nicely dressed young woman, most likely in her late twenties, noticed my stare and promptly reversed the direction of her cart, doing a quick doubletake over her shoulder before turning the corner, I realized the truth. The other grocery store parents (virtually all mothers) didn't see a passionate soon-to-be father. They saw an intense six-foot-two bald man grinning ear to ear at their six- to twelve-month old child. I told Linda about this small problem, which I found just a bit humorous.

"Kermit!" Linda yelled, "Stop scaring women at the grocery store! You ain't right. Good heavens!" She was right, of course, as she *almost* always was.

Growing up, the possibility of being a stay-at-home dad had simply never crossed my mind. I was taught men go to work while women stay home to take care of the house and children, as my father and his father had done before me. Men in my life were absent when it came to rearing children. But deciding to marry the most independent and strong-willed woman on the face of this planet guaranteed I had a different role to fill. While she went to work, I had primary responsibilities at home. While she would save lives, I would raise our son. Feeding, changing, dressing, teaching – I was preparing myself to do it, despite a complete lack of know-how. My go-to was confidence... a nauseating amount of confidence. I told myself that if Linda could impact thousands of patients' lives, then I could raise our son with the same vigor and passion. At least that's what I tried to portray to Linda. Her plate was full enough; the last thing I wanted her to worry about was Spencer and me.

Besides, we knew exactly how to be perfect parents. Perfect parents to dogs, that is. Humans though? Well, we were on the path to figuring that one out for ourselves, which became evident in our adoption announcement.

It was a hand-made card (my first craft of many as a stay-at-home dad) and on the front was a picture of our two dogs looking out the front door. A speech bubble sat above each of their heads: "Is the baby here?" and "Yes, the baby's here!" Then on the back of the card was the same picture, but of their butts from behind, looking out the same door: "Do they have any idea how to be parents to a human?" "Nope. Not a damn clue..."

It didn't matter. We had faith in God's plan for our life, and for Spencer's life.

At the grocery store, I continued to stare (more discreetly) at those little rosy cheeks and tiny hands in the community, daydreaming, until finally, seven months after seeing that first picture, we were on a fifteen-hour flight to South Korea to meet our son.

Before Spencer came into our lives, we considered adopting from Guatemala. Linda's best friend, Andrea, and her husband were in the process of adopting a little Guatemalan girl named Anna Rose, just as we began the adoption process. In the spirit of friendship, we thought we'd do the same. But no matter how much we discussed Guatemala, Linda and I couldn't keep ourselves from going back to Linda's heritage. After a few months of praying, we knew we'd find our child in South Korea.

Seven months later, we landed in South Korea. I could see for *miles*. Apparently, I was one of the tallest people in the country. From the plane to the subway, and all the way to the adoption agency, Linda and I received looks ranging from simple curiosity to discomfort, and as Linda later described to me, even disapproval. (She made it clear that it wasn't because of my attractive baldness, though I joked otherwise.)

I wasn't even aware of these looks until Linda smacked my arm, groaning and mumbling under her breath as we passed a group of women walking toward the agency from the subway. At that time, there was a stigma around military men and mail-order brides, and Linda whispered to me that she would not be perceived as "one of those." I just laughed. Her look of fury and indignation was one of the cutest things. She wasn't too happy about my smile either, which of course just made me laugh (on the inside) even harder.

Inside the agency, despite my drastic difference in size, I might as well have been invisible. It was like the scene from *Return of the Jedi* when the tribe of Ewoks all start humming and bowing to C3PO, thinking he's a god, my wife being C3PO in this case. Every few minutes, another group of women would pile in, their vocal adoration not unlike the collective hum of the Ewoks. To them, Linda was a hero; she was the first native-born South Korean in Holt International's forty-five-year history to come back and adopt a child from South Korea. To them, it signified the child would grow up with a true Korean heritage. Moreover, she had become a successful doctor in America. I just kept asking, "What's going on?" Linda always returned with shushing and annoyed hand-waving.

After an hour and a half, they had yet to bring out Spencer. I felt like I was a new father pacing outside the delivery room, waiting to hear his child's first cry. "Where's my boy? What's taking so long?" I was alone in my torture. Linda was making new friends. I couldn't stop thinking, "where's my boy? What's taking so long?"

Finally, Spencer's foster mom for the first months of his life walked through the door, holding a ten-month old boy with a mop of dark hair and a stuffed animal clenched in his little fist. The strength it took to patiently wait for that woman to put Spencer into Linda's arms was herculean. But to finally see Linda, teary-eyed as she held him close, after months of dreaming together? I would have waited another lifetime just to see that precious moment.

Linda cradled Spencer against her chest. A picture of unconditional love. God's love. A love that would sacrifice whatever necessary to give our child the best life. And He couldn't have found two more willing hosts.

Then Linda turned towards me, a look of mild panic in her eyes that silently yelled: *What do we do now?!*

For the next three days, we booked into a hotel in Seoul, waiting for our return flight. We walked through the door of our hotel room in a daze. Everything was suddenly new and unfamiliar. The corners of beds and tables became sharper, the lightbulbs seemed brighter—even my hands felt too rough for his unblemished skin. We spent the day full of fresh wonder, sharing in our son's wide-eyed experiences.

That night I held him in my arms, bouncing to an unknown rhythm that seemed to calm him. Then an unexpected thought popped in my head: I had to revamp my bucket list. *I'll never get to run with the bulls,* was a particularly acute notion. This fragile infant was now wholly dependent upon me. I smiled. I had to revamp my bucket list. I wondered what else I would joyfully give up for this tiny person. *He* was my new priority. Whatever plans, whatever stupid, dangerous things I'd had on my adventurous bucket list, suddenly became secondary.

Those three days spent watching him crawl across the floor and fumble his way around were easily the shortest days of our lives, without work or worry. We could have stayed in that hotel room for another week, but Linda's three days were up. The hospital had hired another oncologist, allowing Linda time off to get Spencer, but there were limits to what her staff could cover in her absence. As we boarded the plane, our new reality settled in. *I am a dad,* I thought. *And tomorrow, I'll still be a dad.* And the next day, and the next day.

We arrived in Auburn, exhausted and deliriously happy. We spent one more day of Linda's time off together. Watching. Learning. Laughing. Then Linda returned to work, and the house felt strangely empty, even though I now had a ten-month-old child bouncing on my knee.

It didn't take long for that silence to disappear!

Between managing sleep schedules, changing diapers, and washing clothes that took up remarkably little space yet took forever to sort out, I didn't have time to think about much else.

I'd like to say being a stay-at-home parent came naturally to me. I'd like to say that I didn't feel out of place as the stay-at-home parent or as the caretaker of our home. But that wouldn't be accurate.

I would also like to say that I connected with other stay-at-home parents, meeting up with other dads at the park while our kids played on the playground together. Yet anytime I had gone to the park, only mothers sat on the benches, reading their books or chatting with the other moms.

I thought of my grandfather, who didn't learn how to make a pot of coffee his entire marriage, until his wife passed and was no longer there to make it for him. I laughed at the image of him scooping the coffee grounds into the white filter, like it was some science experiment that could explode at any moment. *At least I'm not that ill-equipped,* I thought. But anyone who says God doesn't have a sense of humor either hasn't met Him yet, or has no sense of humor themselves, because I know this: God and all his angels were laughing the day He set Linda Lee Farmer in my path.

We were going to make this thing work, I told myself. And somehow, we did. Linda and I made sure to be there for each other. We each used our unique gifts, that somehow contrasted and complemented each other at the same time, to create the life we wanted for us and Spencer. We learned a healthy marriage was found in making calibrations over time, morphing our expectations of ourselves and of each other, to meet our needs. I believe it's what made our life truly beautiful.

Fast forward ten years. Spencer, now ten years old, sat at the kitchen table with his head in his hands. Linda was yelling, "You're Asian! How can you be bad at math?!" and pointing to the worksheet on the table.

From across the table, I couldn't tell who was more frustrated, the boy who just wanted the relaxed parent to help him finish his homework, or the irate, once straight-A student who had no idea how to motivate her reluctant student.

"Honey," I said, calmly, "I'm not sure yelling 'You're Asian!' is going to change the outcome, no matter how many times you say it." She gave me a dangerous look, but then, *Spencer's* look of "Help me!" urged me forward, be it cautiously. "We need to foster intellectual curiosity."

(That made sense, right? I mean, if you had been standing there, you would have said something like, "Well done, Kermit. You've been reading some negotiation books on de-escalation." Linda hadn't read those books recently.)

"My ass!" Linda sputtered, "He needs an A on the math test tomorrow, not motivational crap! How can he not get it?! I don't get it," she said. "I just don't get it." Then she walked out of the kitchen.

This had been a recurring conversation for the last several months. Since Spencer was old enough to bring homework to the dinner table, Linda felt it her personal responsibility to teach him how to value and find "joy" in education as she had. Obviously, she was the brainiac, so I stood aside, knowing that with Linda's busy schedule, this was one way she wanted to meaningfully contribute to Spencer's rearing. I always wanted Linda to feel she had every opportunity to fill the typical parent role, but it had proven difficult for our first several years as parents. Back in 2009, Linda's practice had continued to expand. The hospital hired more staff to accommodate the extra patient load, yet Linda's level of responsibility never changed. Instead, she was the heartbeat of the organization; some called her the matriarch of the cancer center. Of course, they knew just as well as I did, she liked things done a certain way. But when every decision, small or big, had to be run by the busiest person in the clinic, it didn't leave much extra time in the matriarch's schedule.

This left Spencer and I spending a lot of time together, particularly in the early days. As a toddler, if Spencer got sick, he wanted me to fix it. When he got an earache, he came to me. This drove Linda crazy. Any time Spencer acted indifferent toward Linda, she'd fuss, "What the hell? I'm the one who went to school!" I wanted to comfort her, to show her that Spencer loved her as much as he loved me. But I would have had better luck teaching toddler Spencer swear words than getting him to understand that his preference was hurting his mother's feelings.

Linda faced the same emotions most working moms have at one point or another. Guilt of not being home, guilt of not being there in the moment, and guilt of letting someone else provide for their child. But the acute reality is that if Linda had ever been given the choice between being a full-time doctor or a full-time mom, she would have chosen to become a full-time doctor. It was who she was, and she would never apologize for choosing it. But she wanted the ability to *choose* that role for herself. Instead, she felt trapped, unable to give more at home and unable to say no at work.

I was the parent who changed diapers, did bath time, took out the trash, cooked, and typically cleaned the dishes. Linda did, however, make Spencer's bedtime routine a priority. It was a routine she looked forward to every night after a long day. Reading books, talking about the things mom did at work, brushing teeth. These were the special moments between mother and son that bonded them.

At three years of age, Spencer quickly learned the difference between Linda and me. The things he could get away with when around mom would never be allowed by dad. If we were in an elevator, it didn't matter what kind of elevator, he'd take his little matchbox car and drop it down the gap in front of the door just to see it hit the bottom of the elevator shaft. Then as soon as he heard it crash, he'd cry to mom for a new one.

"Oh honey, don't worry. I'll get you another one," Linda would coo, patting the back of the distraught toddler now gripping her leg. Then she'd look to me, knowing I was the one who would have to go to the store to purchase it. I'd return that look with a silent one of my own that said, *You know he's doing it on purpose, right?* She didn't care. If buying her three-year-old son a new train or car, or whatever he managed to "lose," was the best way to show a mother's love, then she'd happily do it.

After I'd had enough difficult conversations with my wife, I decided to let Spencer continue "pulling one over on mom" as he wished; both were happy with this arrangement. By the age of five, he'd been repeating, "Remember mom said to buy me . . . ." all the time.

In 2003, I came up with the most brilliant idea to woo my wife. (Still a pufferfish.)

Since leaving North Carolina, the place Linda called home for so many years, she would reminisce about her favorite place on earth: the Dean Dome at UNC-Chapel Hill, home of the Tar Heels basketball team.

The stadium boasts 21,750 seats and a ceiling of elaborate steel, painted Carolina Blue, covered by a large, opaque fiberglass roof, which allows the sunlight to naturally illuminate the stadium during the day. Around the circumference of the stadium hangs over fifty jerseys of honored and retired players. By then, I'd yet to see it in person, but Linda described it as majestic and beautiful. So, with the help of Google Images, I was going to recreate it inside our house.

For two months, I planned in secret. Linda was going to be at a conference in Boston for five days, and I had spreadsheets, stencils, buckets of paint, four laser levels, masking for miles, and four college-age artists standing by the moment Linda set foot in her car and drove away. Remember: pufferfish. And how does a pufferfish show love to his wife? By planning the best damn love tsunami she never saw coming.

For the next three days, I kept my powerhouse female volunteers busy stamping stencil after stencil of people along the Carolina Blue walls, filling the recreated stadium with fans while I worked on recreating the steel scaffolding. Thankfully, the room above our three-car garage that was previously an unused loft area, had a vaulted ceiling, which provided the perfect angles to recreate the Dean Dome. Then, for the cherry on top of my perfect gift, I lined the "rafters" with fifty miniature recreations of each jersey, in the correct order. Towards the back of the room, I put the scoreboard that displayed the final score of the last game.

I kept picturing Linda's face as she would walk in: complete visual shock, followed by that beautiful, loud laughter. Then, as a chorus of angels would sing "Hallelujah!" she'd smile at me, speechless, and run into my arms, saying how happy she was to be married to such a kind and thoughtful husband.

A few times before her trip, she caught me smiling for no apparent reason.

"What do you keep smiling about?" she'd ask, and I'd say, "Oh, nothing."

Finally, she came home. The door opened downstairs. "What's that smell?" she called out after shutting the door. She was smelling the fresh paint that coated every inch of the upper room. We heard her footsteps on the stairs, and I couldn't keep the smile from my face. Spencer and I stood next to Nancy, one of Linda's best friends, who wanted to see the big reveal, and waited. "This is going to be so good," I said to Nancy.

Linda walked in. She looked from me to the scoreboard, then wrinkled her nose, like she'd just walked into a room full of Spencer's diapers. "Why did you do this?"

"What—?"

"*When* did you do this?" she asked, looking up at the blue lines I'd painted along the corners to mimic the steel-framed rafters.

I managed to keep the smile on my face, despite my rapidly shifting expectations of how this was going to go. I pointed to the stick figures just past the door on the right. "Did you see these?" I said, gesturing to the cutout faces of our friends and family pasted to the tops of several stamped figures. Each person wore some form of North Carolina paraphernalia or held up a sign that said, "Go Spencer!"

"We never talked about this," Linda said, her voice shrill. "I wanted a movie theater up here!"

The converted room, painted for Linda, was all *set up* to be used as a fun "kids' room."

"Uh, Linda, we need a playroom. I thought—"

"A playroom in the *whole room*? It's a big room!" Her arms were waving rapidly now. "We could have watched basketball up here!"

"Yes, honey, we did talk about that. But that's not where we are right now," I gestured to Spencer who was sitting on the floor, watching this whole exchange. "We have a three-year-old who needs space to play. When he grows up, we can make it into a movie theater. Popcorn machine, minifridge, a little kitchen, the whole works. But right now," I walked over to wrap my arm around her shoulders, "this is what he needs."

Nancy, who'd been as silent as Spencer, piped in, "Linda! Kermit worked really hard on this."

I nodded to her, gratefully. "Thank you." I turned back to Linda, who was still drowning in the remains of my love tsunami. "Did you see the scoreboard?"

She rolled her eyes, turned around, and we all followed her down the stairs. Nancy shrugged, an apologetic look on her face, but I just laughed, shaking my head. *Oh, my stubborn woman.* It truly bothered me not. "A" for effort.

At this point in our marriage, I hadn't yet figured out my wife's aversion to receiving gifts. I knew we both showed love through acts of service. I served Linda; she served her patients. It was our entire life together. But to end the sentiment there would misrepresent, even diminish, the true spirit of my wife's affection. Maybe she wasn't the wife who doted on her husband, or readily gave compliments or showered affection on some random Tuesday afternoon in September. But I really knew she loved me. When I became her husband, she made me a priority when she had no spare time to give. When we adopted Spencer, she trusted my ability to raise our son. When I became a father, she respected the career and other sacrifices I had to make to be a stay-at-home parent. She listened to my opinions. She tried to understand my emotions, even if she didn't share them. She loved me in a way I didn't deserve. Unconditionally.

So, whenever I poured out my heart to her in the most pufferfish way possible, and she'd respond with "it could've been better," I wouldn't get upset. She chose to love some spastic, eager-to-please golden retriever like me, without asking for anything in return. And for that, I would've done anything in the world to make her happy.

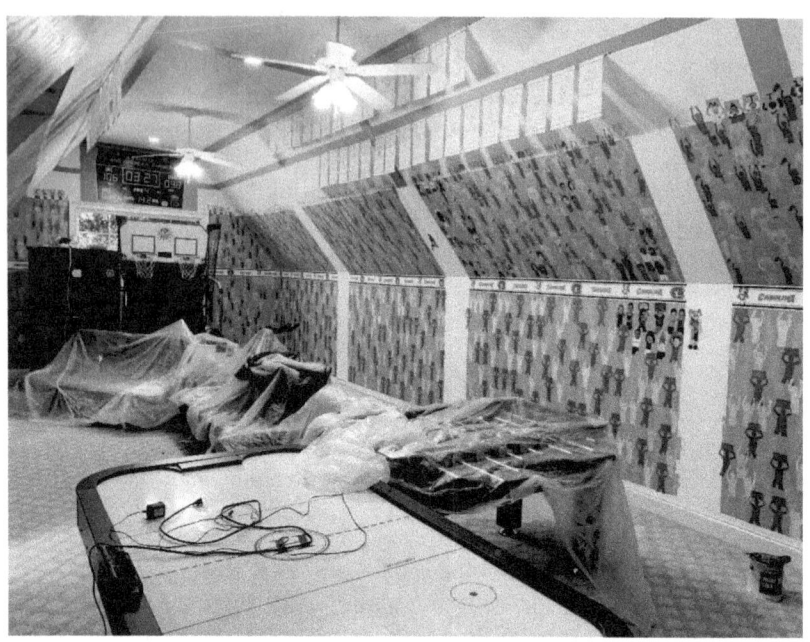

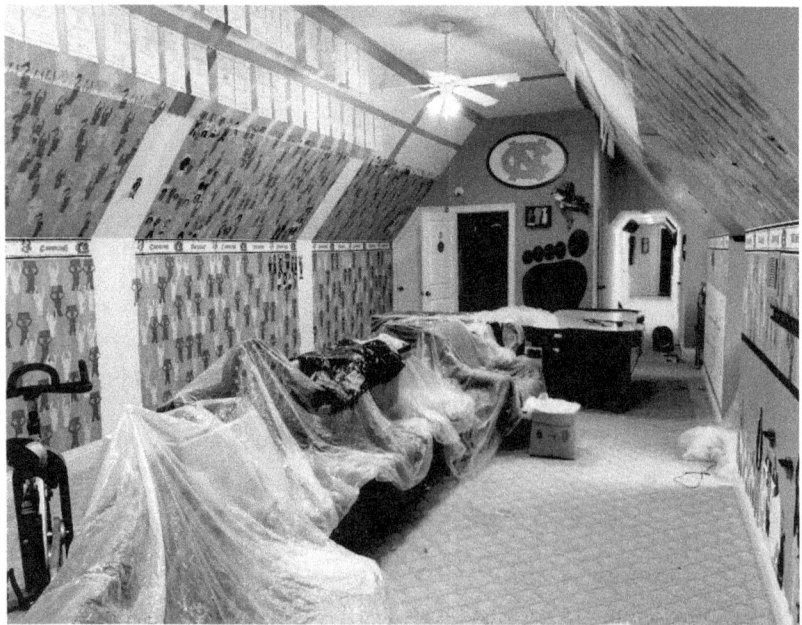

CHAPTER 5

The Spencer Cancer Center

*I*n 2016, Linda visited Chicago and ended up seeing the original production of *Hamilton* in the CIBC Theatre. Though I didn't know what it was at the time, this Broadway rap musical that turned the world upside down[18] became Linda's new love. She drank the Kool-Aid and wanted me to drink it too. "Oh Kermit, you have to see *Hamilton*," she said excitedly the minute she got home. I smiled, enjoying her rare giddiness.

"No, really. We have to get tickets, now! Here, put on the soundtrack," she said, pulling out her phone.

"Linda, I don't want to listen to it before I see it. If the artist would have wanted me to just listen to the music, he wouldn't have turned it into a play. It would be a disservice to the art!"

She rolled her eyes at that. "Whatever!" She groaned. "I really want you to listen to it. You're gonna love it!" She looked up at me with wide, pleading eyes.

"No," I said, pulling my arm from her grip. I don't take saying no to my wife lightly. In fact, I'd rather do anything but say no to her. It's like that line from *It's a Wonderful Life,* where George Bailey says to his girl, "You want the moon? Just say the word, and I'd throw a lasso around it and pull it down." I was George Bailey, and Linda was my girl. But something about seeing her so excited made me that much more resolved not to give in.

Plus, I really did mean what I said about experiencing the show the way the artist intended. For me, the anticipation was more than half the fun. Like

---

[18] Extra points if you get the reference!

foreplay. You build the tension, the excitement of what's coming next, and then—*boom!* You get your socks knocked off. And something told me *Hamilton* was going to blow my socks right off. Linda, on the other hand, was giving me a look that said, "Your foreplay is overrated. Can't we just get to the good part?" She was the kind of person who needed to know what you got her before unwrapping the gift. No wonder she hated my love tsunamis. They were like a gift she couldn't open ahead of time.

For the next several months, she attempted to crack my resolve with the same arguments: "It'll mean that much more when you see it," or, "Aren't you even curious?" She never figured out she was just making it worse for herself. The more she fought for me to listen, the more determined I was to wait. It was like a fun game for me to see how irritated she could get, which of course, made her even more mad, which of course meant I was winning.

Finally, after nearly a year of this back-and-forth, I was ready to end my journey of denying myself, and my wife, the genius of Lin-Manuel Miranda. We sat down in the Richard Rogers Theater in New York; while thumbing through the program, I leaned down to Linda who was buzzing like a kid about to shoot her first BB gun. "Fine, you win." I said in her ear, "I guess I'll listen to the soundtrack now." She glared at me, hitting me hard in the side with her elbow, but she couldn't hide the smile that crept across her face.

A voice boomed through the speaker in a ridiculous posh-British accent: "Ladies and gentlemen, this is your king, George III … Welcome to *Hamilton*."

I think she enjoyed watching the left side of my face more than she enjoyed seeing it for the second time. By the end of the third act, I had a sore spot on the side of my arm from Linda smacking me, saying, "See? See? I knew you would love it!" After the third hit, I whispered back, "Yes, but can we talk after? I'm in the moment, here!" That didn't stop her from staring at me during every shocking moment or smacking my arm when another favorite song would start.

When we walked out of the theater, Linda leaned close, finally releasing the burning question she'd been waiting a year to ask. "So, don't you wish you'd have listened to it before the show?" She thought she had me. That look was pure confidence. She was ready to revel in the "You were right" she expected to hear from my lips. But I didn't answer her right away. Instead, I thought back to the number that shocked me the most, called "Satisfied." It took the previous song's insinuations, story, and choreography, and completely flipped it, mirroring the narrative with a heart-breaking twist at the end. It was *brilliant*.

"Nope," I said, "It was everything I wanted it to be. Actually," I stopped walking, "it was better," I said, smiling down at her. She scoffed, starting to pester me again but I told her to just let me enjoy the moment. Just like her, when she came home from seeing it live for the first time, my eyes were still full of stars, and I didn't want them to dim.

First thing the next morning, I turned on the soundtrack, humming along as I made breakfast. By the time I finished eating, a thought struck me. As a member of the audience, you're inexplicably drawn to Alexander Hamilton. For his charm, his intelligence, and even his bluntness that continuously gets him into trouble. But it's this bluntness, this demand for truth and honest action, that also gets him in the position of Washington's right-hand man, a place of influence. I realized that my absurdly honest and determined Linda reminded me of Alexander Hamilton. She may not have been trying to build a democracy from scratch, but she was building a medical practice, and it too was sloppy and messy, yet somehow still quite beautiful. Both had pitfalls and setbacks, yet neither Linda nor Alexander let the fragility of their endeavor get in the way of what they wanted. Rain or shine, they were committed to making the world a brighter and fairer place.

Following Wes's death, the hospital hired another radiation oncologist to take over Wes's clinic, and though Linda wasn't involved in the politics of Wes's former patients being displaced, she felt for them. They had been attached to Dr. Gleason in the same way her patients were attached to her, and they struggled with being moved to a new doctor.

In the evenings, she would come home in a funk. When I'd ask what was wrong, she couldn't speak to any specific reason; without Wes, things had simply changed. The yin was without her yang. And the entire oncology clinic felt that imbalance. But cancer, a relentless villain, cares not for who defends its victims. It just keeps attacking. So, even in Wes's absence, medicine carried on.

Linda's practice was growing beyond the space the hospital could provide. *Again.* Of course, if she had any complaints, no one would have known. She took what was in front of her and made the best of it. But that didn't mean she didn't see the need for more efficiency, more staff, and in a perfect world, more time.

Within a few months, the new radiation oncologist also saw issues needing to be fixed. From what Linda heard, he approached the hospital to build a free-standing cancer center. The top floor would be for full general oncology services and the bottom floor would be all things radiology. The eventual buildout would include a boutique for women, a chapel, a resource library, and several other amenities that would make the patient experience as smooth and enjoyable as possible. After a few years of meetings and discussions, the name of the clinic had been decided: The Spencer Cancer Center.[19] It was named after its biggest donor, who was none other than E.L. Spencer, the man responsible for keeping Linda employed in Alabama, and the man after whom we named our son.

Situated on over fifteen acres of land, it had the potential to be everything Linda wished her patients could experience, though she didn't put in effort to be involved in the construction. Back when she informed the hospital that she just wanted to see patients while they did the rest, she meant it, and remained true to her word. Even as the 93,000 square foot cancer center was being built, she didn't much care how her office looked, or where her things were located; all she wanted was for her patients to have a comfortable place to sit, plenty of sunshine, and a beautiful view for them to look at while receiving treatment. She didn't care, until she saw how far away the bathrooms were.

A few months later, Linda and I walked into the new center for the first time. "What the hell? My patients are too sick to walk that far! They had one job…just put the patients first." she said, stalking down the hallway. I politely reminded her she didn't have much room to complain when she didn't bother officially weighing in at the appropriate time. But that didn't stop her from bringing up that and a few other issues at least once a week for the next few months. "Why are the doorways so damn small? How are you going to fit a wheelchair through here comfortably? What about emergencies?!"

---

[19] To this day, my son is still convinced it's named after him.

What is obvious to a staff of nurses and a brilliant oncologist with a heart the size of Texas is not always obvious to everyone else.

In the world of medicine, a natural cadence develops between staff. Nurses anticipate what the doctors require before they have to ask. When one medical professional is absent, another fills the role. It's a trust built from years of growth, of seeing the best and worst parts of each other; it's accepting the imperfections of the system while perfecting the practice. Linda's staff had that cadence. From her closet clinic in 2003 to the larger space they moved to in 2008, the staff (much of which was still identical after half a decade) had followed Linda's leadership. They trusted her implicitly, knowing that she would get the job done efficiently and thoroughly.

When they moved into the stand-alone facility, that cadence was thrown off. Either from a lack of organization or a change in efficiency, the staff struggled to manage the extra space. Every few days, her staff pulled Linda aside asking when they would be getting more personnel. She'd tell them she'd talk to the hospital leadership about needing more people, but whenever she did, their response was always something like, "We'll get right on that, don't you worry."

Days, then weeks, went by, and there still wasn't any new staff. Waves of fatigue turned into unnecessary burnout, and it spread through her staff like a virus. Each evening, Linda came home with more staff complaints saying they couldn't handle the extra hours and "all the other crap."

"Everyone's already doing extra. What if they quit, Kermit?!" she asked me, hands running through her short hair. She'd gone to the leadership a few times now, but they'd replied with general hiring concerns of the "candidate pool being slim, right now." Each time I saw her read their replies at home, she'd groan, saying something unintelligible under her breath. But come the next day, she'd have that same smile on, as the matriarch of a cancer center, she never really sought out in the first place.

After a few members of her staff quit, (it was bound to happen, she told me), she feared it would throw off the team's dynamic. But those who stayed knew that to work for Dr. Farmer was to work for something greater than yourself. There were high expectations, and Dr. Farmer's ever-incessant standard of care. It was like choosing to work for Chick-Fil-A instead of Sonic; you know to show up in track shoes because you're about to be put to work. That's what made Linda's team the best. There was an energy, a movement, that invited others to be a part of her mission. While she zoomed across that center every minute of every day, everyone had the freedom to work how they wished, as long as they remained under the umbrella of the ultimate mission: to provide the best damn care possible.

But Linda's definition of "best care" conflicted with reality. In fifteen years of running her own practice, she still fought against the same villain: time. As the medical world became exponentially more digital, patient education remained painfully analog. There weren't tools or resources to expedite information about a disease to the patient; all information was delivered through word-of-mouth.

Take a sixty-five-year-old woman who comes into the hospital with worsening chest pain, a lack of appetite, and a lingering cough. After some tests, the patient is referred to Linda. A lung cancer diagnosis. A full workup ensues. She then explains treatment options, short-term and long-term effects, life expectancy, and which treatment she recommends based on her DNA, genetics, and physical health. After Linda gives the prognosis, the patient asks for Linda to repeat the information to ensure that she, the patient, fully understands. (Remember, of course, that most cancer diagnoses are followed by shock, making it that much more difficult for information retention). Linda spends another several minutes going over the main points of their prognosis again, making sure they fully understand what they're likely to be experiencing over the next several months, possibly years. Then, she makes time to answer whatever questions the patient has. Inevitably, as she answers one question, the patient thinks of another, and so on. Then, somewhere toward the end of that conversation, the diagnosis *really* settles in, and waves of emotion crash through the patient. Now, the patent's logic and understanding of complex medical conditions and treatments, give way to the pure reality of this all. What the patient now needs is comfort. Now, picture all of that needing to happen up to Dr. Linda Farmer's requirements, all within a twenty-minute timeframe.

Linda saw the gaping time-wound in the system. She tried to bring attention to how deadly it was to rush, as this would diminish the trust between doctors and patients. But there was no proffered leniency or grace to spend more time with them. Rather, she was encouraged by leadership to speed *up* her time with each patient.

"Well, that's just bullshit," she'd say, then refuse to budge. Linda believed every patient had a right to the information affecting their life, and it was her duty to share it. Her staff learned from her example.

Over the years, I've enjoyed hosting parties and cooking for the staff and their family members. We always held these parties at Linda's partner's house that was practically built for entertainment. But once the hospital finally hired more personnel, the staff outgrew our annual Christmas party for the oncology team, and we needed to rent out a space to fit everyone.

In tandem with these parties, I over-engineered a cookie giveaway. It started back in 2010. Spencer was only four years old, and just as I was responsible for buying Spencer's replacement toys, I was also responsible for buying Christmas gifts for most people in our lives. Not fully comprehending what I was signing myself up for, I suggested I could bake cookies for a few people as their gift. I made three different types of cookies—chocolate chip, cranberry orange, and a fluffy lemon cookie, and assembled and packaged them all up nicely. They turned out well, considering I was not a baker and didn't particularly enjoy baking.

The following year, Linda asked me—scratch that, *told* me—to make those same cookies, but twice as many. "Of course, honey," I said, putting on my man apron. But, being the pufferfish I am, I turned a simple evening of baking cookies into a full-fledged cookie-operation, in-part, due to my sometimes self-sabotaging mantra, "Anything worth doing is worth overdoing."

I baked the same three kinds of cookies and wrapped each type in a cellophane sleeve for easy shipping in the mail. By this point, I was already in deep, so I thought I might as well make a logo to go on the box. The following Christmas, several hundred cookies went out with our new logo, which included our bakery's official name: The Fox and Two Dudes Bakery. (Linda, of course, was the Fox.[20])

---

[20] She was hot! Could you blame me?

By the fourth year, we were making over 1,800 cookies, sending boxes to whomever Linda told us to (when I write "us," I really mean me. Spencer, a classic boy, rescinded his offer to help after the first dozen). Linda would come home and say, "Make another box for this family, they have the sweetest kids." "Send an extra box to these folks, they're coming to church this Sunday." Of course, as strong tithers, the first 10 percent of the cookies was given to church staff.

We had so many cookies to make, we had to commandeer our church's kitchen for three days. After those three days, I was ready to put on some overalls, disappear into the woods, chew some tobacco, and wrestle a bear with my bare hands to bathe myself in some traditional manhood.

Instead, to man-things up a bit, I put Hot Wheels flames stickers all along the mixing bowls. I told Linda we were doing "manly baking." I imagined I was making sausage, not mixing flour and sugar. I also named my Kitchen-Aid Ol' Faithful, because, thankfully, that little baby stuck with me as my wife would constantly find another hundred or so new cookies for us to make.

At least no one can see me in here, I would think. But no, my *plight* would continue. Much to my chagrin, at our Christmas parties, I was referenced as "the cookie guy."

(If you're reading this, please manifest some Chuck Norris jokes, monster truck tickets, or anything manly to regain what I lost in those days.)

Two years after The Fox and Two Dude (But Really Only One) was closed by yours truly, the world shut down in response to Covid-19. Parents and kids isolated from grandparents, people with poor immune systems isolated from everyone, and Linda isolated us for her patients. "If *you* get sick, then *I* get sick. And if *I* get sick, then my patients *die*," she would tell Spencer and me.

When the only people you see in a day are either receiving infusion treatments and chemotherapy or are recovering from one or both of them, there's little room for additional risk. Linda pulled longer days. Spencer missed his friends. Linda pulled longer and longer days.

We did our best, as did most people on lockdown, to fill our time with meaningful memories. We watched all seventeen Marvel movies, in order, as back-to-back as Linda's schedule allowed.

We were no strangers to movie marathons. Every year, we sat down together to watch all nineteen hours and thirty-nine minutes of the *Harry Potter* films, as well as all eleven hours and twenty-two minutes of the *Lord of the Rings* films. Though it took several weeks, we eventually made it all the way through the Marvel cinematic saga to *Avengers: End Game*. But choreographed fight scenes and cheesy one-liners weren't enough to keep Linda distracted from the reality the epidemic had brought upon the world.

Even when Linda visited her patients, over half their time was spent discussing Covid procedures in an attempt to reassure them the clinic was doing everything they could to mitigate the risks. She answered the same questions over and over again. No, your cancer is not a death sentence. Yes, getting Covid is a risk, but that's not a death sentence, either. Yes, six feet apart is the recommendation. Everything was out of Linda's control, and not even my wife's determination could bring order to the chaos. It finally started to get to her.

We were sitting on our couch one evening after Spencer had fallen asleep. My hands began to rub Linda's scalp, and I expected to hear all about her day of trying to calm overly nervous patients or listen to the latest work drama. Then she rested her hand on mine, stopping me. "I think I have an ulcer," she said in a calm voice. I looked down. Her eyes were still closed.

"What makes you think that?"

"My stomach's been giving me trouble for a while. And I don't feel hungry. Or I just can't make myself eat, even when I am." Her hands came to rest across her stomach.

That *was* strange. In our nineteen years together, I'd never seen Linda leave more than two bites on her plate. Her eating habits were like those of a middle-aged man. She wanted ribs, with a side of ribs, and one more for dessert.

"I was wondering why you didn't finish your dinner. You said this has been going on for a while. How long is 'a while'?" I asked.

"Just over two months. Maybe three, by now." She sat up to face me.

"Hmm, well—" I started, but she touched my arm, stopping me.

"Kermit, it also might not be an ulcer." Her free hand combed back her black hair, the red and blue streaks just visible in the lower light, then offered it to me. I grabbed both her hands, her fingers feeling cool against the warmth of my palms. Then she met my eyes. "It could be stomach cancer."

"Well, this conversation escalated quickly!" I said, almost laughing. It wasn't funny, yet all I wanted to do was laugh. The idea of Linda having cancer was just preposterous. She was fifty-one, ran every single weekend, was healthier than 99 percent of the world population, and spent her time helping *other* people heal from cancer. There was too much irony. *Besides,* I thought to myself, *I'm going to be the one to go first.* After all, she was the smart, responsible, altruistic one, while I was the spontaneous, fly-too-close-to-the-sun guy.

"No," I said, without a hint of doubt in my voice, "you don't have cancer. Your nerves are shot, your schedule is all crazy from Covid and whatever else… It's an ulcer. From all the stress." She blinked at me, eyebrows furrowing into a line, and said nothing. In that moment, if someone had asked me if the sun would rise the next day, I'd have answered with less confidence than if someone had asked me if my wife had cancer. "Linda, it's *not cancer.* So, let's just figure out what's really going on."

She nodded, eyebrows still knitted together. "OK," she said, offering a small smile. It was forced. She was in doctor mode, analyzing her symptoms through the databases she kept inside her brain. I could see her thoughts as easily as the expression on her face; she still thought she had cancer but was placating me.

I may not have had twenty years of doctoral experience under my belt, but what I did have was conviction that I was going to die first. So, unless I got hit by a bus in the next year, Linda had an ulcer. I was ready to bet money on it.

Within the week, Linda was getting test results back. She'd done the tests quietly to not alarm her staff. When her bloodwork came back with some concerning results, she ordered more tests, trying to rule out what she felt she already knew. She began consulting with a doctor in Birmingham.

I knew they were all going to be negative. *She does not have stomach cancer.*

One afternoon, not more than ten days after the first "I think I have an ulcer conversation," the phone rang while we were sitting together in our backyard. The Birmingham hospital appeared on the screen; the results of the latest blood tests were in. Linda rose to answer the call, so I sat up, waiting for the "all clear."

"Hello, John," she said. After a few nods, she put the phone on speaker, and I heard Dr. John Christian say, "--you to repeat the test."

"Oh, don't bullshit me," Linda snapped. "What are you seeing in the numbers?" She was pacing back and forth now. Through some doctor lingo and foreign medical terminology, he told her the blood test came back abnormal. Linda didn't seem immediately distressed, so I took that as a good sign. *OK, another test,* I thought. *Nothing new yet. Just another test.*

"OK ... Mm-hmm ... thank you." She hung up the phone. For the first time in days, there was certainty in her eyes.

My blood turned cold.

"Repeat that test."

She sat down again and nodded slowly.

"I'll repeat the test."

Two days later, the results came back early in the morning while she was at work. Of course, I wasn't there.

"Thank you," she said, then hung up the phone with John. She stood for a moment, then walked to her partner, the first oncologist she had brought on years before. He stood up as she approached, ready for what she had to say.

"Brandon, I have stomach cancer. I want you to be my doctor." Then, without waiting for a response, she added, "I need to go home now."[21]

I was in the garage when her car pulled into the driveway. She got out, still clad in her white lab coat as shut the door behind her. She stood tall. Firm. Like Wonder Woman herself, ready for war. I saw the tears in her eyes.

I couldn't say anything; I couldn't stop swallowing. Over and over again, like the tears that I refused to let fall were running down the back of my throat instead. My hand reached out, grabbing hers, and brought her closer to me. Her hands came to rest on my chest then she hugged me. I was sure she could feel the pounding inside.

"I'm not afraid to die," she said against my chest. It was as much to me as I think to the enemy itself. An enemy so familiar, it was almost unassuming. An enemy I'd dismissed at every turn. And now it was at our doorstep. Yet my wife stood in the middle, like a flame in the dark, burning brightly despite the increasing possibility of extinguishment.

Within the week, Linda was laying down in the hospital's MRI machine. One benefit of running your own clinic is being able to run all your own tests. Once the MRI was complete, she hopped down from the table, walked behind to the viewing area, where she'd previewed thousands of others before, and began analyzing her own scans. She needed to figure out what

---

[21] This was the second time in sixteen years Linda had ever asked to clear her schedule.

stage she was in. Just as Linda expected: nothing. No indication of cancer. I thanked God, letting out a breath. I knew it wasn't going to be serious, stage one if not even earlier than that, but it felt safer to have confirmation of that from a machine. She turned around to look at me, more serious than normal. "I already told you nothing would show up. I don't have enough sugars in my body composition. We're not in the clear yet."

"But it's still something to celebrate, right?"

She blinked, then turned back around. "I'm going to have to do a few more tests."

PART II

Note from the editors: By design, Part I was written in past tense, and Part II in the present tense. We hope this methodology pulls you deeper into the latter half of this story.

CHAPTER 6

The Cancer Doctor Gets Cancer

5/3/21

My Patient Family,

I hope this letter finds you well and in great spirits.

As a patient of mine, you know I've given "the cancer talk" a few times. Truthfully, a few thousand times. This is where I describe what it means. What type of cancer. What to expect during treatment. If you can work during treatment. I'm rather famous for "if you were my relative, I would recommend..." and then, talk to the family.

Today, I get to talk to you as my family about me. I need to let you know I'm stepping away from my practice for a few months as I battle cancer. I'm open and don't mind you knowing I have stage one stomach cancer known as linitis plastica. I feel great other than a little trouble digesting food at the moment. However, I know my treatment ahead is hard and cannot continue the standard of care you deserve as I get treatment that includes chemo and surgery.

I'm writing this letter to let you know I'm unavailable over the next few months. You are in good hands. Your care will continue to be excellent as will mine be at the Spencer Cancer Center of EAMC.

A friend of mine sent the following text of encouragement to me. I think it encapsulates my journey and the many friends today at my side.

"Well marathon partner, looks like we are going to run a different kind of marathon! I am ready to be by your side and support you, lift your

spirits when you need it, plan your water and food stations to keep you hydrated and your sugar levels good, just like the marathon we ran together. There will be rough miles, but then there will be good miles, just like when you discovered pickle juice stops cramps!! I hope that we can bring joy and love to you throughout this marathon. And as you cross each milestone of this process of healing, may we smile and hug each other. I love you. Now let's lace up our new running shoes and keep our pace!!"

As your doctor, and now as a fellow patient, I'm in the marathon with you. I'm lacing up my shoes and joining you in the race. Please know I value privacy at this time. This is best for me and my family.

The Spencer Cancer team will be in touch with you. Please expect some changes to appointments as we all work through this together.

God has a plan.

It takes just over fifteen minutes for Linda to pen the letter. She looks at me, a sad smile on her lips, and I squeeze her hand, her words echoing in my mind for the hundredth time. *I'm not afraid to die.*

She knows all the facts about her condition. She told me that of all 200 cancers out there, stomach cancer is one of three you really *don't* want to get. And that it's not the cancer itself that's the real threat, but the resulting infections that come from having the stomach removed.

We wait together, preparing for Spencer to come home.

I've seen my wife do many things. I've seen her console her patients. I've seen her cry with them and pray for them. I've seen her optimism. In her strange Linda way, she makes them feel safe, somehow at peace with their disease. But I've never heard my wife give "the cancer talk." And I never imagined the first time I'd see it would be on the couch in our living room.

Linda is already sitting down. I can't get myself to sit still for longer than a few minutes, so I stand, resting my hand on her shoulder. Spencer walks through the door, and she tells him to come over and sit down. Then she grabs the hand of our fourteen-year-old son and begins the talk she's given no less than 1,000 times. Her voice is soft, but not quiet. Her words, warm and nurturing. She speaks with ease, and strength, like a lament written as poetry.

She's prepared for his tears when they come, drawing him to her chest as she once did when he was a child. Her fingers run through his hair as she whispers to him. Unconsciously, I think there must be some limit to how much you can be in awe of someone else. Some point in time when you stop being surprised. Well, my wife is living proof of the opposite.

Then a hollow thought comes to mind: *This could be the last cancer talk she ever gives.* The thought makes me shudder and I try to shove it away, but like a snake, it wraps around my throat, and it's hard to breathe. My limbs feel numb as I stand behind the couch, trying to focus, to memorize, every word Linda is saying. I'm suddenly aware of Spencer, cradled up against his mother. I think how this new reality is going to affect his life. Soccer. His grades. It's hard enough being a teenager in this world, in this pandemic. But being a teenager with a sick mom is unthinkable. I join them on the couch, wrapping my arms around them both, and silently pray for a miracle.

The next day, we're back in for another MRI. So far, the only thing confirming any sign of cancer is her blood work. Linda hops off the MRI bed and is around the corner in four seconds. The other doctor, sitting by the computer looking at her scans, moves over as soon as she enters the room. I'm standing behind them, trying to not interrupt their "doctor" talk. I notice Linda's tiny frame looks even smaller beneath her gown. She's lost fifteen pounds. Each time she steps off the scale at home, she says nothing, despite my questions.

I hear the word "clear," and a small jolt runs through me. "So, the scans are clear. They don't show anything?" I ask, trying to stay optimistic. Linda looks at me over her shoulder. "Is there any chance—"

"Dammit Kermit, I told you even before we had the first scan it wasn't going to show anything. I don't have enough sugars in my body."

Right. Not enough sugars in her body. I nod despite not having a single clue what sugar has to do with cancer. But it doesn't seem like the right time to ask that kind of question, so I resume my silent role.

"We're not going to know how bad it is until they open me up and we see what's really going on." She turns back to the screen, though it seems pointless to me now since they don't even show a damn thing.

Today is Linda's first day in the infusion chair. A few days ago, Linda was fitted with a device called a port, a little plastic disc, the size of a quarter. It sits just beneath the skin above her clavicle and connects a small plastic tube to one of her major veins, eliminating the need for further needle pricks. Aside from the initial bruising, she tells me it's painless and is the best possible way to receive chemo treatments.

When we arrive at the Spencer Clinic, I open her car door and wait for her to step out. Despite the cancer center's proximity to Highway 280, the air smells fresh, like wildflowers, pine trees, and cut grass. It may not be a Thomas Kinkade painting, but it's an unusually peaceful morning. I follow Linda as we enter the clinic. They assign her to chair two, located in bay one.

Over the years, Linda harbored complaints about the hospital's chemo bay. They were short-ceilinged rooms in the shape of a box. The walls were painted a cool white, while the harsh lights made everything appear slightly orange. The air was stale, smelling of dust and hypochlorite, and no source of vitamin D entered the room. Patients sat in these rooms for hours at a time, once or twice a week, for months. She saw how it affected the patient's energy, how the light emphasized the shadows beneath their eyes, and under their collar bones.

So, when the design of the Spencer Cancer Center was put on her desk for review, one of the few details she did make time to address was to demand that the infusion room be bathed in sunlight from morning to evening. She wanted every patient to have a front-row seat to nature and the forest just outside.

Nearly half the perimeter of the 93,000 square foot cancer center is made up of ten-foot-tall windows. All five chemo bays face towards the southwest side of the building pressed up against a dense forest where maximum sunlight streams in. Just below the expanse of windows lies a tiered landscape with an assortment of colorful flowers, lush grass, and stone steps. Linda may not have wanted a new facility in the beginning, but even she can't deny how much better it is for the patients. Now that she is a patient, even more so.

I sit in the corner chair, watching the nurse connect the infusion tube to her port. Each patient's chemotherapy treatment is carefully concocted through analyzing several factors: age, health, weight, muscle mass, etc. Linda's treatment, created for a fifty-one-year-old marathon runner, is not for the faint of heart, or body.

I ask if she feels nervous. She shakes her head, then says that doesn't mean she's going to enjoy it. I've seen what chemo has done to Linda's previous patients. Chemo kills both bad and good cells to rid the body of a tumor. Weight loss, hair loss, fatigue, nausea. But even seeing Linda all hooked up, it doesn't feel real yet. Aside from her lack of appetite, the only noticeable difference is her energy; the lack of nutrients is weakening her body. Though she tries to stomach protein drinks, she doesn't like them much. I pack some for today anyway, expecting her energy to decrease even more once we're finished.

Linda's body, mostly made of muscle, is a perfect candidate for chemotherapy (if there's such a thing) which gives me a strange comfort. There should be less risks, though she tells me again and again: "It's not the stomach cancer you have to worry about; it's the recovery from having the stomach removed and any complications that follow." Of course I listen, and nod, and try to remind myself of that. But as the optimist I am, I tell myself, all things considered, we have nothing to worry about.

Sitting in an infusion chair from four to eight hours is about as exciting as it sounds. Most patients bring something called a "chemo bag" often full of items for entertainment. iPads, books, music, or magazines. Linda doesn't get the chance to even crack hers open. Ten minutes into her session, the first care package arrives, along with the first visitor. Then three minutes later, the next one comes. Five minutes later, another.

I stand behind her, waving over each visitor as they ask to come in. Some hide their sadness; others make sure to laugh. It's so good to hear Linda laugh again. The last few days have been tragically absent from that sound.

Several members of the staff are wearing a t-shirt that says "We got this" on the front; they give Linda one to wear as well. We smile at each other, comforted by the solidarity.

With each visitor, there's a unique balance between how they treat Linda as "the patient" and how they treat her as "boss lady." As their patient, they want to give her the best care possible; as their boss, they know she will note every word and detail, and will have something to say about it. But beyond that, she is their family, and seeing her hooked up to a bunch of machines is surreal, even to the other patients receiving chemotherapy.

Imagine looking over your shoulder and seeing your doctor in the same vulnerable position as you. Fighting the same fatigue, taking mini naps just like you. My little force-of-nature looks almost human in this setting, and in some ways, I find myself cherishing the experience.

Around hour four, Linda whispers to me that she's getting tired. I nod, taking my cue as the guard, signaling the remaining visitors to come back at another time. When her breathing turns steady, I release my hand from hers and walk towards the giant window. The sun is hiding behind the trees, casting a shadow across the grass and flowers. Everything is still. Peaceful.

Linda can receive medical attention from anywhere. She can see any doctor she desires. Yet, she chose to stay local, to receive care in her own practice, and from her own team. I found it odd when she first told me she wanted this. I almost argued with her, thinking what I would want for myself if I were in her position. Sitting shoulder to shoulder with your own patients doesn't sound appealing in the least. But she disagreed: "We have the best team! Why would I receive medical attention somewhere else?!" Well, I couldn't argue with that then, or now. Nowhere else in the world could we receive what we have now. This level of care and attention. The level of thought they put behind deciding which nurse would oversee her treatment. What her patient journey means to both her patients and her team members. It's beautiful. "Kermit?" I hear Linda's soft call from behind me.

"Yeah, honey?"

Her hand stretches towards me. "I'm glad we are here. With my team."

I walk over and wrap my fingers around hers. "Me too," I say, bringing the back of her hand to my lips. Her skin is soft and warm. I inhale, breathing in the natural scent of her skin. "I love you."

She smiles, closing her eyes. "I love you too."

Linda's second chemotherapy session follows a similar pattern, albeit with one or two less visitors. She sleeps more this time around, giving me plenty of time. Plenty of time to do nothing, really. I stare out the window a bit or watch Linda sleep, but mostly I watch the folks from across the bay.

In one chemo bay, I see a woman sitting in an infusion chair. She was there the previous week around the same time we were. No one sat next to her then, and the corner chair sits empty now. She's alone. Then I imagine what it would be like for Linda to be alone. Or me to have cancer and be alone in this moment. No one to help you get ready in the morning and drive you to treatments. No one to carry your bag and hold your hand during the transfusion. No one to comfort you as your hair starts to come out and tuck you in at night.

It's a horrible thought. My eyes burn and I try to blink away my blurred vision. I look to where Linda's hand rests in mine, and silently thank God for the privilege to hold that hand.

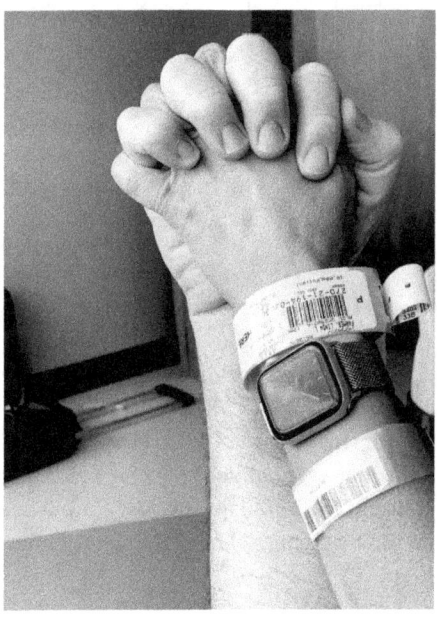

Before opening the cancer center, Linda insisted they include a women's boutique, stocked with anything and everything a woman would need in her hair loss journey. In Linda's early days as an oncologist, she struggled with a lack of these ""extra" resources for her patients. Whether a patient fought to keep their hair as long as possible or shaved it all off at once, Linda knew they needed support. Women would come to her before starting their chemo treatment and ask for the best place to find wigs or hats, and Linda would always point them to a non-inhouse solution. Now, when patients inevitably ask what solutions they have for their hair, Linda directs them to their very own boutique in the center, equipped with a full staff, ready and eager to help.

After Linda's second session, we visit this women's boutique. I let Linda lead the way. Shortly after entering, a gaggle of women whisk her away. Her double status as the founder and now as a patient at the boutique, made her kind of a big deal. I smile, knowing she's in good hands. I wander over to an assortment of wigs. Dozens, in a variety of colors, styles, and lengths. Some are natural brown, or blonde. In front of the wigs are racks of hats and beanies, some with a funny phrase embroidered on the front, others with a heart or a cross. As a bald man, I'm impressed.

I hear Linda's cackle from across the shop. *She's still busy,* I think. *I'll wander around a bit longer to let her have some time to look around.* I pick up one of the display items on the wall in front of me. Then I pick up its twin.

"Wow! Cool!" I say, balancing both items in either hand like a weight scale.

"Kermit! Stop playing with the boobies!"

I jump, spinning around to find the gaggle of women. I freeze, staring directly at the silicone still jiggling in my hands. Linda's back is facing me, but like a million other things, she somehow knew. My face feels hot. A defensive "What...?" comes out of my mouth. The women break into fits, some with polite giggles, others in shameless hoots of laughter. I can't help but laugh along despite being caught red-handed.[22] Now, Linda's looking at me, as I continue to look down at the undulating silicone models, then fondle them, exaggerating my hand movement, "These feel great, honey." The stern look

---

[22] My editor wouldn't let me write "boob-handed."

on her face now becomes downright lethal, but I force myself to shrug, casually replacing the display items back on the wall.

Then, like I always do when I'm in hot water, I get an excellent idea. One that will either make my wife laugh or earn me a bruise on my arm. I scan the wall. *Bingo.* I look over my shoulder to make sure Linda's back is to me, then maneuver across the store like a child trying to hide from his mother in a department store.

I pop out directly next to Linda. She takes one look at the dark brown bob-cut wig sitting on my head then lets out a loud, "YOU!" but is unable to hide that radiant smile.

CHAPTER 7

I Can't Carry Your Cancer, But I Can Carry You

*M*any people consider me to be an optimist. I've been called the love child of Willy Wonka and Rambo, which I quite liked. I'd charge hell with a water pistol if deemed necessary. I mean, look at who I married. The hardest-working, no-bullshitting, most infuriatingly remarkable woman created by God and I've yet to figure out how to do anything nice for her without getting my head chewed off.

In more ways than one, I see my wife as Frodo Baggins (in spirit more than physicality, though her height is arguably close to that of a hobbit), and I see myself as Samwise Gamgee, Frodo's best friend and ultimate defender in *The Lord of the Rings* trilogy. While my wife, tasked with carrying the one ring up to Mount Doom, is trying to save the world one patient at a time, I'm standing beside her with a pack of supplies on my back, there to console, encourage, support, and even fight if necessary. But as much as I aspire to be like Samwise Gamgee, the character whose optimism urges them on to Mount Doom, I find there is a limit to my own. It's starting to fray around the edges, like a single string pulling loose from a woven tapestry. Each small pull, unraveling the picture more and more.

There are plenty of culprits pulling at my patience. But one that I can't stand? The casual **"How are you?"** being constantly thrown in our direction. Visitors, nurses, doctors. Every time, "How are you?" seem to be the first three words out of someone's mouth. I keep thinking, *What kind of question is that? Do they mean, how are we emotionally? Physically? Financially? Spiritually? Do they have three days to stand here while I actually tell them about our plight, or would they like me to come up with some five-syllable answer that moves us along to the next topic?*

101

It's calories burned on wondering how to navigate, calories that I must burn because the asker wouldn't and Linda can't. She doesn't have them.

After four "how are yous," I start a mental list of useful questions for anyone else in this situation:

> *Are you feeling better or worse since last week?*
>
> *Are you sleeping OK at night?*
>
> *How is your spiritual health in this journey?*
>
> *What needs does Spencer currently have; can I help with him in any way?*
>
> *What are you most looking forward to this week?*

These questions are quantifiable, and they force the asker to burn their calories.[23]

But it's not just the questions. It's also the "Big C" face. Have you ever seen it? The face that says, "Oh you poor thing, you have cancer, you must be miserable. Your fight ahead is going to be so hard." I almost appreciate the sentiment. But none of us in this situation—as the caretaker or the patient— ever, *ever* wants the Big C face if we or our loved ones *actually have the Big C.* Believe me, we're aware. We don't need anyone reminding us. Instead, make us smile, or laugh. *That's* the type of energy we *do* need.

Linda's fifth and last chemo session before her stomach removal surgery is, thankfully, straight forward. We're now past the first round of chemo, but a new chapter is about to begin. Surgery.

By the time we make it to the car, Linda's winded from the walk. I hold her hand, watching her drift off in the passenger seat. I reach to turn on the radio but think better of it; she needs the sleep.

I put the car in drive. *Samwise Gamgee would know better what to do. Kermit, you're not trained for this. You're not prepared for what's coming.* I

---

[23] Trust me, I've now had lots of friends who've been on a cancer journey, themselves, or with loved ones. Use these questions instead of "How are you?"

exit the parking lot. I merge onto highway 280. I take the turn towards our home. *How can you be a good father and a good caretaker? You don't know how to be what everyone needs you to be.* I pull into the garage and turn off the car. I don't remember the drive home. We are here now, so I must have made the right turns, but the whole thing is a blur. Linda's still sleeping, so I settle in my own seat, about to let my eyes close, but I hear Linda shift in her seat. I look over and she's smiling tiredly. She closes her eyes again, then says, "We should go inside."

Once Linda is on the couch with her favorite blanket tucked around her legs, I excuse myself to the dining room where all her meds and equipment for her treatment are scattered across the table. My shoulders feel sore. *I need to be there for Linda. I need to be here for Spencer. I need to do a lot, and I don't have the strength.* I let out a breath, then bring my hands together, leaning my elbows on the counter, and pray. I ask God to take away my negative thoughts. I ask for strength. For wisdom. For Him to heal my wife.

This journey has been harder than expected, and I know the road ahead will be even more so, though I don't know by how much. But compared to what others must go through, wrestling through their healthcare experience without the know-how or sociomedical capital of my wife, I thank God we at least have that. My heart breaks for those patients who aren't as lucky as we are. An echo of a scripture comes to mind:

> "Therefore take up the whole armor of God, that you may be able to withstand in the evil day, and having done all, to stand firm. Stand therefore, having fastened on the belt of truth, and having put on the breastplate of righteousness, and, as shoes for your feet, having put on the readiness given by the gospel of peace. In all circumstances take up the shield of faith, with which you can extinguish all the flaming darts of the evil one; and take the helmet of salvation, and the sword of the Spirit, which is the word of God."[24]

It's time to answer the call. I *am* Samwise Gamgee. If I have to carry my Frodo up Mount Doom, I will find a way.

---

[24] Eph. 6:13–17 (English Standard Version).

I turn off the water, then bend down towards the shower drain and pick up a clump of dark hair. Linda comes into the bathroom and says nothing as I wrap the clump in tissue paper. I toss it into the trash to join the others that have been clogging our shower drain for the last several days. Neither of us wants to look at it, so I look at her instead, gently cupping the side of her face. Her eyes search mine, and she nods. "I know," she whispers. "It's almost time."

I walk into the living room and see her sitting on the couch. Her face is turned from me, but I can tell something's off. Her shoulders look tense, like she slept wrong and is afraid to turn her head.

"Everything OK?" I ask, kissing her head.

She scoffs lightly, waving her hand, then lays it atop mine on her shoulder. My other hand cradles her head in my palm. Her hair feels soft and thin.

"You know, I'm kind of an expert at shaving heads," I say in a casual tone. I receive a reflexive eyeroll. I continue, chuckling: "Being bald and all, I've got the tools for it." Then, I bend down, bringing her hand to my lips. I kiss her knuckles. "When you're ready."

I know Linda has counseled hundreds of patients who've lost their hair. And, particularly for women, finding hair in their pillowcases, stuck in their hairbrushes, or clumped in their shower drains, the experience is just heartbreaking. My wife usually tells women to adjust in phases: A crew cut first, then, once 60 to 70 percent of the hair has fallen out, shave it.

Today, it's her turn.

She sits on the edge of the bathtub, facing away from me. I connect my phone to a mobile speaker on the edge of the sink. My hands find her shoulders, rubbing gently, as Nat King Cole croons "(I Love You) For Sentimental Reasons." Our wedding song. I had picked this song over a month ago for this exact moment.

I think back to our wedding day. . . thirty-one-year-old Linda and myself, dancing in small circles. I have one arm wrapped around her back, the other holding out her smaller hand. We're swaying to the music as I sing off tune

104

with Cole. Linda's hair perfectly frames her flushed cheeks as I bend down to kiss my new bride.

Then, back to today. I look down at that hair, now dyed with streaks of red and blue. So contemporary. Even in the yellow cast of our bathroom lights, it's beautifully dark. I run my fingers through it for the last time, breathing in the soft smell. *"Please give your loving heart to me,"* I belt out with exaggerated vibrato and imperfect pitch. *"And say we'll never part."* I bend down to kiss her temple. *"I think of you eveeeery morning."*

She smiles, eyes closing. Her hands find mine on her shoulders, squeezing. I squeeze back, then grab the clippers sitting next to my phone on the sink.

Our song is a perfect portrayal of our relationship. We didn't fall for each other because of our looks or because we had a *spark*. I saw her heart, and she saw mine. She could have married anyone. She almost did marry Chris. I wonder absently if she would have been happy with him. And if she had married him, would she be in this situation right now? I'll never know the answer to that, nor should I care. But, I do. I tell myself that God chose me to be here, now, cradling her head, singing our song, and making her laugh.

She flinches slightly as the cold clippers brush the side of her head. "Ready?" I ask. She nods once and I turn on the clippers. I shave away from her face, gently gathering the loose hair in one hand. I bend down, kissing the newly shaven spot, singing louder now to drown out the buzz of the clippers.

"I love youuu." Shave. *"For sentimental reasons."* Kiss. *"I hope you do believe me."* Shave. *"I've given you my heart . . . ."* Kiss.

I pull away the last strands of hair, adding it to the dark pile next to me on the tub. I brush off a few pieces of cut hair that had landed on her shoulders and help Linda to her feet. She walks over to the mirror.

Her hand rubs the peach fuzz-like hair from her forehead to the base of her skull, breathing in. As she breathes out, a brief smile touches her lips. Perhaps not much of a smile, but a quirk of acknowledgement. She is now in her patients' shoes. She understands another part of their pain. Their fear. There is no more empathizing; she can relate to their experience in its entirety. And strangely, she looks proud of that fact. A fresh twinkle of resolve enters her eyes, and all I can think is how much I love her for that.

I draw her in towards me as I turn the shower on, helping her rinse off the clinging pieces. Once dried off, we immediately get into bed (we both had agreed it was best to do this at night).

Linda falls asleep quickly while I lay beside her, hugging all of her one hundred pounds to my chest and close my eyes. I can still see her face looking in the mirror for the first time, eyes moving over the now visible parts of her scalp. Calculated and clinical. Not something I'll soon forget. Like a frozen image imprinted on my mind. She didn't cry. I wasn't expecting her to cry, but I wouldn't have been surprised if she had. As a man, I have no idea what it must be like to lose what most women deem part of their femininity.

Linda told me once that after a patient shaved their hair, that they felt more tired, more irritable. Like they actually had cancer. She said, once someone looks like they have cancer, they often feel like they have cancer. Looking at Linda, I was struck by that same thought. Before, no one would have known. Now, she has cancer.

I close my eyes, feeling the soft fuzz brush my cheek. I fall asleep.

Another chair, another office, another doctor discussing things only Linda understands. It's two weeks until Linda's stomach-removal surgery. For over twenty minutes they go back and forth. After hearing something about how he'd "find out" what to do during the surgery, I interject.

"Wait. . . you're telling me you don't even know if you'll need to do this surgery until she's on the table? And you're talking about removing the stomach, then attaching the large intestine to the bottom of her esophagus?"

He nods casually, like attaching an intestine to an esophagus is as easy as taping two straws together to form a longer straw. "Yes, that's how we need to do it. The surgery should take no more than an hour, maybe an hour and thirty minutes. I would plan on being here for at least a week after for recovery, maybe two."

We continue going back and forth, mostly for Dr. Farmer's husband's understanding. I ask him the same questions over, and he patiently answers them, again. I look to Linda for confirmation. She's in full doctor mode. "It's called a gastrectomy, or partial gastrectomy, depending on how much of my stomach needs to be removed." *Sure.* Then she explains what all that means for everyone in the room who didn't go to school for an extra decade. (Everyone, meaning me.) Then, she turns back to Dr. Christian. "So, how do we prepare?"

They start talking in doctor-babble. I drift off. *Damn, we'll have to be away from home for two weeks in Birmingham, where the surgery will take place. That's over two hours away from Spencer. OK, we'll have to call—*

"Oh shit," Linda says, interrupting my thoughts. *What just happened? What were they talking about?*

"You're right," says Dr. Christian. "You are not healthy enough for surgery. We need to get some weight on you first. You need to be stronger for the journey."

I look at all 102 pounds of Linda, which, even for her two-by-four frame, was low. In the last month, her ability to consume calories, food or protein drinks was decreasing each day. Whatever was blocking her stomach was making it impossible for any food to pass through.

"Are there any other options?" Linda asks, her tone flat.

Dr. Christian shakes his head, then says, "TPN."

"Shit!" Linda yells.

"Wait, what's TPN?"

She looks at me with that same resolve she had looking in the mirror. "I'll tell you later. Time to go," she says, dismissing me with a wave. We get up to leave. I'm about to argue, but she's already out of the room, click-clacking down the hall.

Back in the car, I blurt out, "Linda, can you *please* tell me, your husband by the way, what's going on with you? What in the hell is TPN?"

"Sure." Cue doctor mode.

"I'm going to have a tube placed in my port and my nutrition is going to come from a bag of liquid that is hanging on my back and it's going to feed me twelve hours a day, every day. And you're going to be the person that has to hook me up to it and change out the bags."

"OK, I'm going to need you to unpack that for me."

She gives me the same spiel again, verbatim. I decide it's better to not ask her to repeat herself a third time, so I nod, pretending her second explanation somehow made more sense than the first. I still don't know what a TPN backpack is, but figure I'll know sooner than I'd like to.

Within a few days, Linda receives her TPN backpack. We are assigned a home health nurse, Sara, who shows me how to change the nutrition bag, how to access her port just beneath the skin above her clavicle, and how to insert the nutrition tube. She gives me a hands-on tutorial for the first two feeds to "ensure I don't kill Dr. Farmer." Though Linda, who is watching every step of my training, also makes sure I don't kill Dr. Farmer.

But once we get home, the pressure really comes on to put the non-medical guy to the medical test.

Consider this: on someone's best day, say a student attending a college lecture, they retain around 17 percent of what's being taught to them. In the last few days, I've received a lecture of my own, but if I only remember 17 percent of how to administer TPN, . . . there will be some major problems.

For example...upon receiving the "Total Parenteral Nutrition (TPN)," which is a bag of nutrients to be put directly into Linda's vein, I must first make sure it is stored in the refrigerator at 35°F. Then, to get the mixture ready, I must follow the steps *exactly*, which seem to begin in a somewhat straightforward fashion:

Take the TPN out of the refrigerator for two hours before use so it becomes room temperature. That makes sense.

Then, they continue on:

Find a clean workstation like the kitchen or dining table to prepare TPN mixture.

Thoroughly clean hands.

Make sure you have all the equipment you need.

Normal stuff, right? Sure. But there are four pages of it. And that's just the setup instructions. Then there are other directions, for other potential issues, like how to add medication to the TPN[25] (two pages).

Then there are other instructions about setup, insertions, protective coverings, etc. Here are a few excerpts:

How to: Attach the Administration Set to the TPN Bag.

- Take the protective covering (pull-tab) off the TPN bag spike port and put it on the sterile barrier. **Do not touch the exposed end or let it come in contact with anything.**
- Pick up the TPN administration set. Hold it below the sharp end of the spike tip in one hand and remove the protective covering.

How to: Insert tip of the administration set into spike port of TPN bag.

- Hang the TPN bag on an IV pole or hook. If you have a portable pump, you don't need an IV pole.

How to: Squeeze the chamber of the administration set.

- Open the roller clamp and let the solution fill the entire length of the tubing, including the filter. The filter is a safety device that traps air bubbles and any particles while the solution is running through the tubes. Make sure that there is no air trapped in the tubing.
- When the tubing is filled, close the roller clamp. Thread the tubing through the infusion pump, using the instructions on your pump as a guide.
- Clean the CVC connection at the end of the lumen with an alcohol wipe.
- Flush the lumen that you'll be using for the infusion with 10 mL of normal saline (see instructions in the "Disconnecting the TPN Tubing and Flushing Your CVC" section).
- Remove the protective cap from the TPN tubing.[26]

---

[25] https://www.mskcc.org/cancer-care/patient-education/home-total-parenteral-nutrition
[26] Ibid.

Remember, *someone's life is in your hands.*

All this is added onto the healthcare journey of someone, a caretaker, who's loved one is receiving TPN because they're already between a rock and a hard place. And they have to do all this with precision every twelve hours, around the clock, every day, for weeks or months on end, without mistake.

Utterly exhausting, physically and mentally.

We're up by 4 am and in the hospital by 5 am. It's been two weeks since I first learned about TPN. Now, we're back in Birmingham for Linda's surgery. She's 112 pounds. Good, but she wanted to get to at least 115.

We sit in the waiting room, listening for Linda's name to be called. It's been an hour. We're holding each other's hands, brushing thumbs over knuckles, touching lips to cheeks. I cradle her head in my hand as her temple rests against my shoulder. We talk about silly things, and even soft, intimate things Linda would normally shush me for.

"Linda Lee Farmer," the nurse calls out from the door. I help Linda to her feet, give her a kiss, and watch as they wheel her to the back. "The procedure will take between forty-five minutes to an hour and a half," the nurse informs me.

"Thank you," I say, returning to my seat.

The time passes quickly. It feels as if it's only been thirty minutes of pacing before I hear: "Kermit Farmer." I look up. "The surgeon is ready to see you." *Oh, thank goodness. It's over now.* I start to breathe easier.

The nurse brings me to a small room to the right of the main hallway. It's about seven feet by nine feet with two chairs in the middle of the room. The surgeon is standing in front of a door on the opposite wall.

"How did it go?"

"I was surprised. I really was," he says, rubbing his jaw.

Surprised? There must be less cancer than we thought! I open my mouth to ask a question, but he speaks first.

"Linda's organs are matted together. I've managed to get one of her kidneys free, but the other is still stuck to her liver, and both are stuck to her stomach. I've spent a good amount of time trying to separate them, but I truly was not expecting that."

My previous relief vanishes. "Is she going to be OK?" I ask before I realize how dumb of a question that is.

"We're doing the best we can," he says. *Not really an answer, but OK.* I thank him, trying to think of what question I could even ask.

"Hey Kermit," Dr. Christian says, "I need your help to make a decision."

"About what?"

"About the next steps. How do you want me to proceed?"

I wait for him to keep talking.

He doesn't.

I replay our short conversation from the last ninety seconds. I finally stammer, "Are you—wait, are you saying you stepped out of surgery to speak with me, while Linda is still on the table?"

"Yes." *His tone is so casual. Why is he being so casual about this?*

I talk. "And now you want me to decide what organs to remove on Linda's behalf?"

"Yes."

My heart bottoms out in my chest.

"Shit." Silence bangs in my ears, louder than drums.

I continue to stare at him.

"Um—"

"OK, OK." he says, grabbing an expo marker, "Here is Linda's stomach." He draws a crude outline of a human body with squiggly organs on the white board next to us.

"Here is her liver, which is attached to her stomach. Her kidney should be here, but it's stuck to the liver. So, all of this," he says, drawing a circle around the expo-person's abdomen, "is stuck together like glue." He looks at me, interlacing his fingers together on the word "stuck." He caps the marker, returning it to the board. "So, what do you want me to do?"

I try to focus despite being acutely aware that she's on the operating table with her organs exposed. I ask again, stalling. I have no idea what to do:

"You've come to me to decide what to remove… a kidney, some of her liver, and her stomach…and we need to make this call right now?"

"Yes, that's what I need to know." I look between the surgeon and the crude drawing, feeling suddenly nauseous.

"I have to make a call."

I dial Linda's godparents, both in the medical field. I put them on speaker to allow the surgeon to weigh in. Tom and Vicki are calm and relaxed, which is what I need right now.

I think back to a conversation I had with Linda early on in her career. She was struggling to let a patient stop fighting. She'd come home in fits, asking me how she could convince her patient they could beat it. I told her, "Everyone should get to choose how they meet their Maker." Ideally, it's our choice, and no one else's.

Linda's always had a strong stance on her patients' quality of life. No matter the scenario, she'd say, if someone cannot be saved, then do nothing. She advocates for the best possible solution. If chemo won't increase their chance of survival, she won't compromise their health.

After some back and forth, Tom finally gives me what I need: a decision.

"Kermit, you and I both know Linda. She wouldn't want to live a life with three missing organs. There's no quality of life in that. I suggest they do the original surgery, sew her back up, and Linda should decide the next step."

Lord, thank you for Tom Hunt. "Thanks, Tom." I hang up the phone, feeling a shred of comfort knowing the surgeon isn't going to remove half my wife's major organs.

"If she wants to go through with it, she can do a second surgery," I say to Dr. Christian, "but for now, remove the cancerous parts of the stomach as intended. We'll worry about everything else later." He nods once, then disappears behind the door to meet the team of personnel waiting for him to return with a plan.

I stalk back to the waiting room. I call someone. I talk for a while, bullet-pointing everything that just happened. I try to keep the shake out of my voice. *Keep it together, Kermit. No reason to lose it yet.*

I don't have a reason to be angry, so why am I furious? How did my hatred for cancer get any deeper? No, maybe this isn't anger or hatred, but fear, fear disguised as anger. I shake my head. I'm not listening to the other person on the end of the line. I mumble some form of goodbye, then hang up.

I start walking towards the front desk to ask for the nurse. A man, about my size, stops me. He mumbles something, then reaches out and hugs me. Surprised, I pull away. Then another stranger comes up. She touches my hand and says, "I'm so sorry," and another hand touches my back. A third person stands behind me. I hear three simple words:

"You're so strong."

The moment is too much for me. "Excuse me," I say. "I'm sorry, I have to go. . ."

But there's nowhere I need to be. *But I can't just stand here,* I think. *All the thoughts of Linda's organs, the surgeon's drawing, her laying on the table? That'll kill me. I have to keep moving.*

They all heard me on the phone, I realize. *Now, they're offering something beautiful and kind. But that's not what I need. I need my wife to be healthy. Happy. I need to know what to tell Spencer when we get home.*

I look around, and more people start to offer me words of encouragement. *My wife needs me to do something, but I have no place to go.*

I stand in the corner as the medical team begins to wake Linda up. Linda blinks.

"What'd we find out? What's my status?"

"Uh. . ."

"Kermit, what did John say?"

Holy crap woman, how are you this intense already?

"They removed two-thirds of your stomach." Then, more words about the messiness of her organs, filling in details as best as I can without an expo marker.

She listens, before falling back asleep, saving me from my unsavory explanation. *I must have done a good enough job, because she seems satisfied!* I think.

Two hours go by. When she wakes up, she doesn't remember that conversation, and for that, I'm thankful. This time, I'm better prepared to handle the conversation. I explain the complications of her surgery, telling her about my call to Tom and Vicki, and their help in deciding what to do. She reaches for my hand and squeezes it before letting go. I exhale, now fully believing I made the right decision.

Linda starts asking about her biopsy results and blood work, so I let the nurse take over to answer all her questions. "What are you looking for?" I ask. She tells me she needs more information on the metastasized cancer. Before long, the nurse gives Linda a smile, "I'll be back with answers as soon as I have them," then disappears around the corner.

We are alone again. Six hours go by.

A nurse finally walks into our room with some information. "Good news, Dr. Farmer. Your margins are clear."

"What's a margin?" I ask.

"Shut up, Kermit!"

"Yes, dear."

"Good morning."

It's Dr. John Christian, and he's pretty chipper for so bright and early, and our first morning in the hospital post-surgery.

He starts talking. About three minutes in, I've gathered this much: her Biopsied lymph nodes are clear and cancer free, which is a shock to us all. I look at Linda, slightly bouncy in my giddiness. *Cancer free! That's the important part, right?!* She smiles, but she's more fascinated than excited.

"Wait, so if—

"Kermit! Stop asking questions!" she says.

That's right. The adults are talking.

But then Linda asks my next question before I can. "What's making my organs stick together then?"

Dr. Christian smiles. "Retroperitoneal fibrosis." *Right, retro parrot fibers were my first guess.*

Linda exclaims, "Retroperitoneal fibrosis. Really?! Huh!"

"What's retroperitoneal fibrosis?" I ask, turning to Linda. [I actually think I got the pronunciation correct. Good job Kermit!].

"A byproduct of the cancer, like a discharge or mucus that builds up on the organs and fuses them together, like glue."

Then, back to herself: "Huh, retroperitoneal fibrosis. Interesting."

Only Linda Lee Farmer would find that "interesting" in such a circumstance, I think, raising my eyebrows. "We can handle this," I say, as much to myself as to her.

She smiles, nodding, then goes back to the adult conversation.

I say a quick prayer:

Lord, thank you for Tom, who told me not to remove my wife's perfectly functioning organs.

CHAPTER 8

The Wound That Never Heals

*W*hile in the hospital, I start sending updates on Linda's health status. I create ten different group chats, about 150 people in total, and write quick blurbs about how Linda's feeling and how Spencer and I are doing. Then I fill in the gaps with some much-needed humor (though Linda doesn't much agree).

I've learned by now there is an art to dark humor jokes. You need just the right amount of sarcasm, some hyperbole, even some self-deprecation (my specialty). Just like any art, some people get it, while others scoff and shake their heads, offended. This of course doesn't stop me from making jokes at my wife's expense.

I'm sitting in a chair near the one window in our room, smiling impishly to myself. Linda is sitting up slightly in the hospital bed. She glances over at my chuckle.

"What are you laughing at?"

"Oh, just my superb wit and charm," I say, giving her a wink. She curls an eyebrow at me. "Here, read this. I just sent this out," I say, handing her my phone:

> "Six days out of surgery and I officially want to smother my wife with a pillow. We're back to where we were so everything is great!"

Linda's head snaps up, glaring at me. "You did not just do that."

"I did," I say, still grinning. *If I'm going to send a message to over one hundred people each week, or as needed, I'm gonna do it with honesty and radical*

117

humor. "You were a pill yesterday," I say, smiling happily. "Not in a bad way but in a Dr. Farmer way. Thinking one step ahead, not happy with the status quo. You seemed like yourself, and that is worth celebrating. A return to normalcy before we blow this joint." She reluctantly agrees, now grinning a bit.

"Also, I really did want to smother you yesterday. So, I'm glad you lived through it!"

She looks over at me. *Oh, if only I could capture that look on camera! It would take the front-page spot of my "Kermit really stepped in it" photo album.*

If I don't cause shenanigans now and then, who am I?

Eight days after surgery, we are finally driving back home. Linda's asleep in the passenger seat, and I hold her hand thinking of how much we have to tell Spencer. I shake that thought away, not looking forward to explaining the details.

Upon getting home, Linda gives Spencer a long hug. "Hey mom," he says, smiling. He tries letting go, but she tightens her arms around him, eyes squeezing shut. Even at fourteen, he towers over Linda. He's strong for his age. He's grown so much. He finally releases her, and they share a smile only shared between mother and child. It's good to see her smile at her son. It brings some color back to her cheeks.

For our bedroom, I had ordered an adjustable double bed frame, and was planning to turn one bed in the opposite direction to be able to see her face. The more I can look into her eyes and hold her hand, the better I can help when she's in pain. And when she's in need of a good laugh, which is every hour of the day as far as I'm concerned.

Spencer and I help Linda to our bedroom, then retreat back to the kitchen to catch up about his friends and his schoolwork. He tells me about his time at school while we were away: uneventful, somewhat boring, nothing to report. I think of asking for more details, but realize his brevity is probably just him wanting to know about his mom. So, I tell him. Not all the gritty details, but enough. As usual, he handles the news well. Though we've talked on the phone, this feels more personal. I send him back to our bedroom, encouraging him to spend time with his mom before she falls back asleep.

The next day is surprisingly and pleasantly calm. Though Linda's soreness is higher than the average stomach-removal patient's.

Standard stomach removal surgery takes over an hour, but in Linda's case, they spent hours just scraping and prying, trying to get her organs unstuck from one another. The surgeon told Linda it would be a tough recovery, but she already knew that. She had thanked the doctor then whispered to me that a little soreness wouldn't be the end of her.

On our third day home, Linda complains about a dull pain in her stomach. I ask her what kind of pain, considering a great deal of it is expected. She tells me it feels as if something's off.

"With all the digging around they did, I doubt it's anything abnormal," I say, gently touching my palm to her stomach. I put my arm around her shoulders, giving a light squeeze.

"Hmm," is all she replies.

It's 1 a.m., our fourth day of being home.

"Kermit, something's not right. I need to see what's going on under the bandage," Linda whispers to me, waking me up.

For a moment, I consider fighting her: I really don't want to remove the gauze unless absolutely necessary. But she has a knowing tone to her voice, almost like panic, and Linda *never* panics. My body comes awake in a second, and in another ten seconds, I'm out of the bed and kneeling in front of her in the bathroom underneath the light.

I start to remove the bandage. The incision runs from the bottom of the sternum to the top of her belly button, closed with sutures. She winces as I pull the last of the tape and gauze free, then gives me a single nod as I place my thumbs on either side of her distended belly and apply the slightest amount of pressure. A surge of yellow pus breaks through the sutures. The thick discharge hits the floor and runs down the slope of her belly. I look up at her, a mixture of shock and horror on my face. She lets out a terrible cry. I look between the floor, her stomach, and her face, unsure if I should reach out and hold her as I kneel in front of her. Gently, I place my left hand back on her belly, further from the suture this time, and apply the slightest pressure. More pus comes pouring out and I look up, her face a mirror of my own.

In less than eight minutes, I have Linda into the car with a towel wrapped around her middle as I pull out of the driveway. I make two phone calls: one to Grandview Hospital in Birmingham, telling them we're on our way and need to see Dr. Christian immediately, and another to Amy, a very close friend, asking her to sleep on our couch until Spencer wakes up. For the first time, I hear real fear in Linda's voice. I talk about whatever comes to my mind to distract us both. We make the two-hour drive to Birmingham in an hour and ten minutes. The towel around Linda is drenched through and unable to soak up more of the fluid continuing to seep from her stomach. It looks slightly green.

I feel helpless. I fend off my own doubts. *Not now! Not after all we've been through!*

By the time we get to Birmingham, for the first time, Linda is in patient mode instead of doctor mode. I've always looked to her for directions, for orders, but this time, it's different. She exchanges a few words with the nurse before we check into a room. I take my place, pacing.

The team of nurses quickly removes the sutures, then begins clearing the sticky liquid pus still pouring from her wound. I—and Linda, I might add—grimace as they do so. Her breathing is short and quick. Subconsciously, my breathing mirrors hers.

The hole in Linda's belly is now fully exposed as she looks at the ceiling. I wince, looking at her, back to the wound, then back at her. The infection removal lasts over thirty minutes. Finally, Linda looks down at her stomach. The wound is fileted open, exposing her raw human tissue. Her eyes lock with mine, both of us knowing what this means but not ready or wanting to accept it. This moment in time, our shared look, burns into my memory, like a gruesome scar in both our minds, forever.

Each time Linda moves to adjust herself, more pus comes from the bottom of the deep incision. The nurse puts on the dry replacement gauze, but they saturate within fifteen minutes and need to be replaced with more. Each gauze change, Linda's face grimaces, both from the pain and the inevitable path ahead.

"It's an infection, but what kind of infection? How bad?" Linda asks out loud, but really to herself.

She sits in bed with bandages from the bottom of her chest to the top of her hips. She is staring at the ceiling, I imagine, running through every possible scenario, most likely exhausting herself trying to figure all the variables in her head.

Dr. Christian walks through the door, interrupting Linda's monologue. "You have a fungal infection, and there's multiple bacteria within the wound that's causing the excess discharge."

"Oh shit." Linda says, looking away.

"What does all that mean?" I ask, looking from her to the surgeon.

"It's a nasty fungal infection," she says, waving me off.

The next ten minutes I spend watching as the doctor and the surgeon speculate between one thing and the next. Back and forth, back and forth, like watching a Wimbledon tennis match. Even with her stomach cut open and a painful infection, she's as sharp as ever.

I stare at her, imagining her brain rhythmically whirring as she listens to his next hypothesis, calculating her own ideas. She smiles suddenly, laughing at something he says. It was like a single ray of sunshine breaking through the storm clouds circling my head. Somehow, I manage to smile too. Just as I experienced her pain the night before, I mirror Linda's energy. I have no idea what they're talking about, but it's becoming even clearer (as if I need more evidence), that Linda is brilliant. And if there's anyone who can find humor at a time like this, it's her. Or me. In that way, we are a team.

With an active infection, they can't risk sewing or stapling the wound. It would only trap and worsen the infection. She explains what it will mean for me as the caregiver. Either her wound will heal on its own or it will need to be surgically closed once the infection goes down, but in the meantime, I would need to change Linda's bandages every four hours to aid in eliminating the infection. *At least we have a plan now*, I think. A strategy, her meds, and one reluctant, on-the-job, nurse-in-training (me).

Over the next three days, the nurse shows me how to change Linda's bandages. After each step, she asks me to repeat everything back to her. I feel as if I'm playing a real-life game of *Operation*. Holding tweezers with gauze, dabbing as lightly as I can to soak up the pus, cleaning with saline, then dabbing again to clear the wound. But instead of a buzzer going off and a nose flashing red, I get "Kermit!" whenever I push too hard or hit the tender walls of the wound. My knee-jerk reaction is to say back, "What?!" which doesn't help much. After several rounds of this, the nurse looks at us with a smile, "You guys are too much."

"She's too much!" I quip back, "I'm perfect just the way God made me." This earns me chuckles from two of the three people in the room (I'll let you guess which two).

By the end of the lessons, I feel I should be awarded with a handshake and a piece of paper. Something to say, "You've earned this." I suggest this idea to Linda and the nurse, arguing to both that I've progressed to the final stage of becoming an honorary nurse. For some reason, she and the nurse are less humored by the idea when I ask, "Where's my honorary degree?" which only makes it more humorous and absolutely necessary to me. . . .

Dressing changes are stressful for both of us, neither of us knowing what will be under the bandage each time we remove the gauze. We hope to see clear liquid, almost like water. But whitish clear is not so good; yellow is bad; yellowish green that looks kind of like snot, is really bad.

Each time, I lay her down flat on the bed and get my materials in order on the bedside table. I run through the procedure in my head, then put on the latex gloves, sometimes with gusto like a doctor on some melodramatic television show: "I need you to bend over and cough." This usually earns me a grin.

On top of scrutinizing the kind of discharge, we compare the color and texture to the previous dressing change from four hours ago, as well as the dressing change from four hours before that, hoping to see improvement over time. Identifying a positive or negative trend. When it's bad, we offer hesitant smiles, neither of us wanting to anticipate the worst. When it's good, I learn it's best not to say anything. Each time, I can see just moments before she does, so I try to refrain from showing anything but a neutral expression, knowing she reads my face.

For three weeks, we exchange the bandages every four hours; her wound refuses to close and the skin around the edges is bright red, meaning the wound isn't closing on its own. Then, the pus comes out darker than expected, and it's time for another trip to the hospital.

We go through this cycle again and again over the next few months. Infection. Hospital. Recovery. Home. Infection. Hospital.

Each hospital visit we discover a new bacterium and are sent home with fresh bandages designed to draw out whatever new infection resides in Linda's wound. Our one comfort is being able to stay, not just at any hospital, but at Linda's place of employment.

I wheel Linda up to the sixth floor and we are greeted with a warmth unique to my wife's presence. They understand the responsibility of caring for Linda here. Like when a celebrity sits down at a restaurant and the entire wait staff argues over who gets to serve them. It's one thing to know how much I would do for my spouse. It's another to experience over a dozen people on staff willing to do the same. It is beautiful, and equally heart-breaking.

Once Linda's admitted, I joke with the nurses that there's "no pressure here," despite knowing they feel the exact opposite. They're used to the clickety-clack of her heels using the emergency exit stairwell instead of the elevator to go between floors. They're used to the barking that always gets people moving. Like a racecar pitstop, everyone knows their role and does it without getting in the driver's way.

It's equally surreal for Linda and me, with her now as the patient being attended. In some ways, I find it comforting to get a break from TPN bag exchanges and dressing changes. It feels good to have others help keep her alive. Mostly while Linda recovers, I ask questions about my duties at home, ensuring I'm doing everything right, and get excited whenever I'm taught a new skill or hack I can use at home. When I get too excited, Linda chimes in, "Kermit! Let the nurses do their job!" to which I respond, "Woman, I'm learning over here."

Being married to a doctor myself, I have the highest possible respect for doctors. But *nurses* deserve just as much respect. When leadership is needed, or decisions need to be made, call a doctor. But when real help or knowledge is needed, you call a nurse. Every time.

For a time, our life seems a bit easier at the hospital. Less factors to consider, more time for Spencer to visit, despite Covid preventing him from visiting as often as he would like. He tries to follow along but it's hard for a fourteen-year-old. Hell, it's hard for me to follow along.

It hurts having him twenty minutes away. It hurts even more to go a week without seeing him for each hospital admission. But like the good kid he is, he stays focused. He does his homework and keeps going to soccer practice. It's especially hard watching him watch Linda. Sometimes when he visits, she's asleep. Linda has told me to wake her when that happens, but each time, I leave it up to Spencer to decide. Some days, he lets her sleep, and I don't blame him one bit. Talking about school or soccer seems trivial to him, but that's what Linda asks him about. Somehow, all conversations matter, and at the same time, no conversation really matters.

Every fifteen minutes, Linda's up again, hitting the refresh button on the computer screen, scanning tests and charts. My wife has many virtues, but patience isn't one of them. And every fifteen minutes, I'm telling her to sit back down. "Linda, you've got a lot going on here. Just relax, I can hit 'refresh' for you."

And what do I get for my noble pursuit of taking the best possible care of my wife?

Grrrrrr. "You're not HIPAA compliant!" Meaning: I'm not legally authorized to hit refresh and scroll through the results on the hospital-owned device.

After a few months, Linda's wound is not progressing as needed or as anticipated, and she stops producing adequate urine. We continue to change out her TPN bag every twelve hours, and her pus continues to drain from the wound without much difference, except her loss in weight, but even with receiving fluid calories around the clock, nothing comes out.

When that same shred of panic returns to Linda's voice, we're readmitted into the hospital that afternoon, and Dr. Dansby is consulted. A tall, formidable no-nonsense kidney doctor who knows Linda well. "We need to find out why your kidneys are failing, and time is not on our side," he says.

By this time, I've learned to let the doctors get all their doctor-talk out of the way before I interject and start asking questions. But this time, the problem is scarily straight-forward. Dr. Dansby informs us that during her surgery, her kidney was compromised from the scraping and pulling required to get it unstuck from her other organs. Now, months later, her kidney is going into failure. All we can do is wait for more test results to see how her kidneys will respond.

I thank Dr. Dansby and wheel Linda out of the hospital. "We're not in the clear yet, Kermit." I nod.

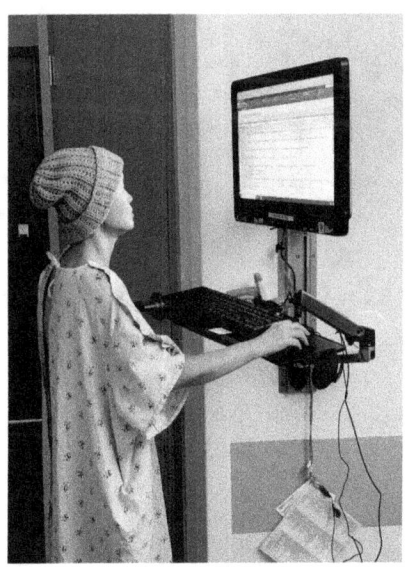

I have a four-hour timer to change Linda's bandages. We joke to each other, whenever we change her bandages or TPN, that it's time to make the donuts. If the pus is clear, we're clear. If it's not, we might be back in the hospital.

Two weeks later, and the pus is still not clearing. Linda continues to lose weight, and renal failure (lack of urine output) remains problematic, and that evening, we're back in the hospital. Dr. Dansby walks in through the door, and once again, I let the adults speak. It's gotten easier with time, knowing when to ask questions, and when to get out of the way, the latter often being the best option. I wait until Dr. Dansby leaves to ask Linda, "Hey, what are you thinking? Is kidney dialysis something you want?"

She looks at me, jaw firm. "I'm not going on dialysis. It's a miserable life. If I go on dialysis, I may never get off. It's a horrible way to go." This is one I understand: If a machine works on behalf of an organ, that organ doesn't always return to working order on its own.

We stare at each other for a time. "You have to get dialysis if that's the only way," I say, firmly. She closes her eyes, thinking. Silence. I wait, tapping my shoe against the floor. More silence.

"Linda."

She opens her eyes, staring at the ceiling for a few seconds, then looks at me, jaw clenched, tearful. Angry. *Oh, no,* I think. But I don't just think it. I say it.

"Oh, hell no," I say, feeling heat rise to my face. "Linda, a kidney is not going to take us out!" I stand from my seat, waiting for her to say something. She watches me pace in front of her, wordless. I stop pacing to point a finger at her stomach, "This is not how your book ends," then resume pacing.

For years, Linda's told me there is a turning point for every patient. The point when a patient loses hope in the fight. A point where they lose sight of the end. All they can see is where they are. Even when Linda tells them they have more to give, even as she speaks words of courage when they have none, little can be done to change their mind.

When that moment comes, and the conversation with Linda is had, she comes home to me, weighed down by their decision to stop fighting and imagines everything she could and should have done to change their mind. And in those moments, I would remind her, again and again, that everyone has a right to meet their Maker on their own terms. But you know what I never imagined? Needing to tell my wife those same words.

"Linda, you have a right to meet your Maker when you are good and ready," I say, coming to the side of her bed. "But please, not a kidney." I bring her hand to my lips, feeling her soft skin. "Fight this. Please." I blink, trying to clear my vision, but all I see are her small hands gripped tightly in mine. "Please," I say again. I clear my throat, waiting. Finally, her hands squeeze mine back, and she nods.

"OK," I breathe out, kissing her hands again. "OK."

All the lights are off inside the hospital. Patients lie sleeping in their beds. The machines monitoring the sick, the recovering, and the dying, beep quietly, undisturbed by the silence. I am sitting in a hospital with several hundred people. I have my wife sleeping next to me, her nurse standing on the other side of the door, not twenty feet from me, and yet I feel alone. Subconscious thoughts wander through my brain, each memory or thought fading as quickly as it appears. I think of how empty my life would be without Linda. I wonder how our son will cope, how I will cope. And suddenly, our nineteen years spent together seem unimaginably short, and in desperation, I silently ask for just one more year. Just one more.

No one prepares you for this. The feeling of helplessness that sits in your gut like you swallowed a ten-pound ball. The outward numbness you show to others that contradicts the raging emotions clashing inside of you. The ache that radiates deep in your bones from wanting to take on the burden of their sickness. I suppose no one can truly prepare you for it.

I think the strangest thing about this loneliness is that it comes in waves. Some hours feel strangely normal, like the world hasn't shifted three degrees off its axis and all hell has broken loose. Some hours, you're able to laugh with them, and hours or days, you don't see the bags under their eyes or the protruding bones of their wrists.

But other hours, in moments of crisis, you're filled with doubt. You doubt your ability to be the person you need to be for your loved one. You doubt their ability to pull through. You doubt that God's in control, that He hears your cries begging Him to take away their sickness.

Those hours and days, where even God seems quiet, are the loneliest.

Most days, good or bad, lonely or not, feel slow. Whatever test result you're waiting for, whatever procedure you're waiting to start, has been put at the bottom of the draw pile. No matter how much you beg the nurse for information, they give the same spiel: "Don't worry, the doctor's on it. Just sit tight, we'll be back with more information soon." I don't blame them for it. Being married to a doctor, I know how it goes.

Yet when one is met with scarcity, it's all that holds your attention. Those who are hungry fixate on their lack of food. Those in a hurry focus on the lack of time. Those without information, well . . . .

But there's an irony to scarcity. When you finally receive the thing you've been craving for so long, it hurts. Like when the long-awaited food sits heavier in an empty stomach, making you feel sick. Time, once precious, feels suddenly meaningless. And as that train full of long-awaited information hits you in the gut, you find yourself wishing for the bliss of ignorance.

For a brief moment, I imagine how many others in the world have experienced moments like this. The anger, the helplessness. I imagine other caregivers beside hospital beds, single parents struggling to raise their kids, even someone desperate to find a job.

For the first time, I am utterly afraid, and I don't know what to do. So, I watch Linda sleep. I follow her steady breath rising and falling, mentally tracing the lines of her face, down the length of her frail body beneath the white bed sheets. I've come to enjoy watching her sleep. She can relax in moments like this, and I get to experience it. No stomach pain. No thoughts of future chemotherapy. Just the peace of unconsciousness. No wonder cancer patients sleep most of the time: it's their one reprieve. I wonder if that's what patients are longing for when they've decided to stop fighting, the peace of eternal sleep.

I rest my hand over hers, thinking what I wouldn't do to take it all away. Absorb the physical pain that everyone sees Linda going through, and the emotional burdens few see— the weight Dr. Farmer feels to be the perfect patient. I lean my forehead against the bed's guard rail, and close my eyes.

Lord, I have served You, and I have served the one You gave me. Somehow You deemed me worthy to have a woman like Linda. But she has so much more to do. So much strength left to give. Why Linda? Why not me?

Thirty seconds go by, or three hours. Eventually, I fall asleep to the sound of my wife's breath.

It's 3 o'clock in the afternoon. I'm dancing down the hallway of the hospital like an absolute buffoon. Linda's nurse is with me, and we ask a tech to follow us with my phone, recording as I jump and whoop down the hall of the sixth floor. I can't think of a better way to tell all 150 people (the number of folks I update each week) that my badass, tough-as-nails wife is getting discharged from the hospital today.

A week prior to me choreographing this celebratory video in the most pufferfish fashion, Linda responded amazingly well to dialysis two separate times, which removed the toxins from her blood. Her kidneys finally agreed to do their damn job and cooperate with the medical team—no arbitration, no union revolt. Linda's urine output went up in conjunction with her blood work. In total, all the signs needed for us to go home. God is finally answering our prayers.

So, in celebration of the moment, for both myself and Linda's weekly updated group of fans (who have been receiving nothing but negative news lately), I send out a video of me, dancing like David before God, to the classic 1959 hit, "Shout," by The Isley Brothers. [27]

But I don't let my shenanigans stop at the hospital. As I get Linda into the car, I tell her we are swinging by the Spencer Cancer Center to let her team visit with her. It's been too long.

I go through the whole building, telling people she's in the car and encouraging them to go visit her (so long as they still follow Covid protocol of course). I stop to dance with some nurses and a few doctors to sing, "My wife's been discharged today!" By the time I return to the car, I'm drenched

---

[27] To see this video, look at the QR code at the end of the chapter. You know you want to.

in sweat and grinning so much my face hurts. Linda laughs, rolling her eyes, and takes my hand in hers.

As we pull away from the center, I thank God. I thank Him for Linda's now functioning kidneys; I thank Him for the staff taking care of her; I thank Him for this miracle of all miracles; I thank Him for the cloudless sky and the fresh grass; I thank God for bringing us to this moment after six months of fighting.

My enthusiasm is somewhat nauseating to the patient, but she doesn't try to stop my giddiness. Instead, she asks, "Why are you so happy?"

"Because we dodged a bullet!" I practically yell. "I'm just so thankful."

"I weigh eight-five pounds, Kermit."

I nod, hearing her, but all the while, saying to myself, "This is it. We really did it. If we can just get her organs to cooperate, if we can get the infections to clear, it's all going up-hill from here."

So, in a matter of hours, we're back to taking it day by day, hour by hour, changing bandages, exchanging TPN bags. Making the donuts.

In *Hamilton*, there's a song towards the end of the play, in which Alexander Hamilton reflects back on his life. He's experienced moments of pure hell as well as moments of amazing victory; finally, after many years of work and turmoil, he experiences a sense of peace. Like in the eye of a hurricane. He doesn't know when or how it will end, but he knows it is a fragile thing, needing to be cherished. My wife and I enjoy two weeks in the eye of our hurricane. Two weeks of hope, two weeks of peace. Two weeks of, "We made it" and "Praise God for this miracle." Two weeks of softer smiles, longer touches, deeper inhales and exhales of each other's skin and clothes.

But we are in the eye. And the eye always passes.

From Kermit: If you want to see the video I made of me dancing at the hospital in celebration of Linda coming home, scan this QR code. If you don't enjoy it, let me know, and I'll send you a free consolation prize.

From the editors: He's joking. After our own viewing of the video, we felt compelled to request the free consolation prize. It's another video of Kermit dancing.

CHAPTER 9

18 Days

D octors are always seeking the balance between science, faith, and the
sheer willpower of the patient. I have so many memories of Linda laying
with her head in my lap, watching her brain factor in the limits of medicine,
the limits of her care, and the limits of the patient. It's a delicate dance,
advising when to fight, when to fight *like hell*, and when the data tells you
the fight is futile. Delivering such news to a patient requires professionalism,
grace, and above all, confidence in the final decision. These are always the
hardest decisions for her, or any oncologist, to make. Hoping it's the right
call, each and every time.

It's hard enough helping the patient understand it's their time to stop
fighting, convincing them that quality of life is still important in the end. It's
another, even harder in most cases, trying to help their caregiver understand.
Patients feel the exhaustion of the fight; even if their mind isn't ready, their
body knows. But caregivers can't know. Often, the weaker their patient
becomes, the more strength the caregiver summons, as if their energy can
sustain them both. It's like a cruel balance scale, designed to never find true
equilibrium.

We are admitted into the hospital. Again. This is the eleventh time in ten
months, and the balance tips. Linda's kidneys are weakening again but this is
not the biggest problem in the moment. It's her liver. It's shutting down. The
infections refusing to clear, a strong contributing factor. Battling cancer is
like swimming against the tide; each treatment, each stroke, brings you closer
to the shore, despite progress being painfully slow. Battling cancer *while
fighting off infection* is like having just enough energy to keep your head
above water, but not enough to swim to the shore. How long can you tread
water before your body, or your mind, decides it's easier to drown?

When we return home from the hospital, I help Linda settle into bed. I adjust the frame so she is sitting comfortably, then collapse onto my side with a huff.

"Kermit, I've made up my mind," Linda says from across the bed, "I cannot recover from this." A declarative statement. No questions needing answers. No "what ifs" left to consider.

"My body is not cooperating."

I try to summon the words, even one word, but my tongue fails me. I stare at her, unable to get my eyes to focus, so I close them instead.

"I cannot heal... We have tried, and my body will not allow it," I hear her say. I think of the thousands of patients to whom she gave this same speech. She'd sit them down, much like I am sitting now, and say to them, "It's your time. Your fight was beautiful, but you need to stop fighting now." Only, she isn't telling me to stop fighting. She's telling herself. I have no choice in this. I wonder how long ago she must have decided this, only to tell me now.

Linda knows her probability of survival, and the quality of life ahead of her if she keeps going. I do too. But what if *I'm* not ready to stop fighting?

"Plus," she continues, "I'm still losing weight." Her tone is even. *She came ready to battle me on this,* I think. She had quite the speech ready for me.

I hear her words in my head again. *I cannot recover from this.* I shake my head, still unable to open my eyes. *I'm not ready.* But if I fight her on this, if I ask her to prolong this purgatory any longer. . . it would tear us both up. She's right. It's time.

"OK," I breathe out, opening my eyes. But no. "Dammit, we can do this." I look in her eyes— those dark eyes that still hold the power to bring me to my knees. "Honey, I'm with you. OK? I'm with you all the way." I scooch down the length of my bed and wrap my arms around her, careful not to squeeze too tightly. I pull back and gently cup the sides of her face. Her eyes are bright despite the fatigue obviously plaguing her, and she smiles tenderly.

I feel a dull pain in my lungs as I think of Spencer. I try to breathe through it, but there's no relief. What am I going to tell him? *How* am I going to tell him? I know Linda will want me to speak with him before she does.

I kiss Linda's cheek, then go back to my side of the bed. I close my eyes once more, and ask one final, silent, desperate prayer for strength. Not strength to carry on, but strength to let go.

The next morning, I've told Spencer of his mom's decision. How? Later, I'd try to recall exactly that—how it happened. I wouldn't know, exactly. How does anyone go about telling their fourteen-year-old son that his mother, while still alive, is choosing to stop living? How had I? I'd search my memory to recall the scene. Every time I tried, I would see Spencer and I sitting on the couch. I would see my own lips moving. I'd look into my eyes. From my face, I could always guess the words, but I could never overhear. The volume was always set to zero. I see mouths moving and tears falling. Father and son hugging. But no sound. Perhaps God edited the scene such, to save me from the memory. The kind of memory that sticks no matter how much you try to scrub it away or replace it with happier ones. He who is outside time, would allow the memory of that conversation to become a bruise that continually blooms a deeper shade of purple: leave it alone, and the pain is dull; poke it, and the pain is sharp and intense.

But with time, bruises fade, as the memory of how I told Spencer.

"I need to write a letter to my patients," Linda tells me. I stand up to retrieve some paper and a pen, feeling profoundly proud that she still thinks of others first.

I've watched her write a thousand times before. *I know her handwriting so well,* I think as I watch the pen scribble away… and this will be the last time I ever get to see her do it.

January 27th, 2022

Dear Patients,

Cancer is fickle.

Back in May, when I first wrote a letter to you, we thought I had Stage One stomach cancer. I had 4/5th of my stomach removed with surgery.

We did not know at the time I also had retroperitoneal fibrosis (RPF). This caused my organs to stick together which was problematic for the surgeon – leading to many complications thereafter.

Unfortunately, we did not remove all of the cancer. I have active cancer now with no treatment options. This letter will reach you after my passing.

I cannot thank you enough for all the cards, letters, and support. I could not respond to all the outpouring of love. My family felt your presence in every moment of the journey.

With cancer, we are all in the same storm together, but in a different boat. Please hear me when I say cancer is not a death sentence. You might be surprised to know many of my patients are still alive from 18 years ago when my medical practice began. They are doing well, healthy, and living their best life. This is what I want for you. You must navigate the seas physically, emotionally, and spiritually. This will serve you well and give you an authentic purpose day in and day out.

God knows the plans He has for me … and for you. All attempts to understand God's Plan does nothing but minimize His Purpose. Our Creator did not give us the ability to answer the "why" questions. The Bible says in 1 Corinthians 13:12 "We don't yet see things clearly. We're squinting in a fog, peering through a mist. But it won't be long before the weather clears and the sun shines bright! We'll see it all then, see it all as clearly as God sees us, knowing him directly just as he knows us!"[28] I find comfort in knowing my questions will be answered soon.

If you pray, pray for my son and his continued development as a healthy teenager. My heart is heaviest for him. Also pray I get front row seats to a few UNC games. I'm guessing TVs won't be needed anymore. Heaven holds so many privileges we can't even conceive what our creator has in store for us.

---

[20] The Message translation.

The next day, I have to tell all 150 people on the update chain what Linda has decided. Not only them, but her family, her friends, the staff of the hospital, the staff of the cancer center... It feels like I'm writing the last page of a long journey that's taken ten months to write. They've traveled with us, mourned with us, celebrated and prayed with us—how does anyone pen the last page of this kind of story? I wish it didn't end like this.

Despite my loud human thoughts on injustice and unfairness, and through divine intervention alone, I sit down to write Linda's choice to her group of supporters. It details her long fight, the epic battles, triumphs, and losses. I write of Linda's strength, her never-fading humor, and that ever-present smile she blessed everyone with.

I finish the text message, hit send, and stand. I stretch longer than needed, then look over at Linda laying in the bed. She's wrapped up tightly in a fuzzy robe with the hood around her face.

"Let's be practical for a minute," she says, returning my look. "The TPN bag will run out soon. Let's not refill it." I try to hide the physical (and emotional and spiritual) pain from this request. She doesn't mean to be jarring, but she always had a gift for getting to the point. I just remember saying, "I will honor your request."

Watching that TPN bag is like watching an hourglass for twelve hours. Each hour, getting a bit emptier, until there is nothing left. Once I remove the empty bag, it's like the beginning of the end; a new clock, now ticking in my head.

> *"Cancer is fickle...Unfortunately, we did not remove all of the cancer. I have active cancer now with no treatment options. This letter will reach you after my passing."*

On Wednesday morning, I receive a call.

"Hi, this is LeAnn with Compassus Hospice—"

I know that voice. There is no way... "Wait–LeAnn. LeAnn Cox?! No way."

"Yes," she says, a smile in her voice. "Is now a good time?"

I can't believe it. Of all the hospice nurses, we get Linda's first receptionist. "Well, that's a God thing," I say. "Yes, please, come on over."

A half hour later, I'm wrapping LeAnn in a bear hug, holding her closely. "The alpha and the omega," I say, pulling back. "You were here at the beginning, and you're here until the end. Thank you for coming."

She smiles, "I wouldn't miss it for anything."

I bring her to our bedroom where Linda's sitting propped up in our bed. She takes a seat, grabbing Linda's hand. Within the span of a minute, they're headlong into a conversation as if they're simply catching up over a cup of coffee. LeAnn talks about her daughter's braces. Linda asks about her latest Instagram posts, laughing over all the things you'd never expect someone on their third day of hospice to care about. *Lord, I don't know how you pulled this off. But thank you.*

A half hour later, LeAnn finds me sitting on our couch. She settles down next to me with a funny expression. In her sweet Alabama accent, she relays a conversation she had with Linda. "Kermit, she looked me right in the eye and said, 'I will be the one directing my care.' And of course, I said, 'Yes, ma'am. Whatever you want.'" She laughs, wiping tears from her eyes. I laugh too, not surprised by my wife's insistence.

LeAnn continues: "I have to say, most patients I see want nothing to do with that paperwork. Not Linda. She practically had it filled out before I asked."

"So you see, nothing's changed," I say, "Always stubborn. Always the doctor."

LeAnn's smile falters. She reaches forward, grasping my hand in both of hers. "I need you to know what an honor it is to be here. Linda shaped who I became as a nurse all those years ago. I could never repay her for that." Tears creep into both of our eyes. LeAnn sniffs, taking a breath before continuing. "I can't come close to giving her what she gave to all her patients. But I will give her all that I have. Until her last day."

"Thank you, LeAnn."

On Sunday, we invite everyone from the office to come visit her between 2 p.m. and 5 p.m. Spencer stands at the door, welcoming each person into our home. I don't know what to imagine having a slew of forty-five medical team members saying goodbye in sequence. Whether it would be a tear-jerking experience or not. But as professionals of the cancer center, who are more acquainted with death than anyone, they have the professionalism and decency to wait until afterward to show outward mourning of the loss of their friend and colleague.

I feel my own need for a sense of professionalism. These men and women aren't just visiting their fellow doctor; they're visiting family. I guide them in and out of Linda's bedroom, ensuring each one gets enough time with Linda before she becomes too tired. They take their turns one or two at a time, sharing joyful memories, filling the room with much needed laughter and jokes. I thank each of them for making what could have been one of Linda's hardest days into one of the most special, marveling at the dedication it takes to do this, day in and day out. I am reminded once again just how lucky we are to have Linda's staff in our lives.

I cannot thank you enough for all the cards, letters, and support. I could not respond to all the outpouring of love. My family felt your presence in every moment of the journey.

Over the course of Linda's life, she loved sending letters and cards any chance she could. She made the perfect pen pal. When there's a birthday in the office, she's already picked out a card and written a little note, as well as included a gift card to their favorite place. Does she ask around to find out what gift card to get? Does she reference a calendar to know whose birthday is when? Of course not. Linda not only knows her previous staff's birthdays and favorite places to eat, but the birthdays of every staff member at the Spencer Cancer Center along with the birthdays of all previous patients. You could tell that woman what you ate for breakfast on the first Sunday of November, and six months later she'd remember.

The next afternoon, I check the mail and find another stack of cards addressed to Linda. I bring them up for her to read, and watch as her face moves from laughter, to pain, to a mixture of both. Even now, I can see the burden she feels. She isn't thinking about herself, wondering what she is missing out on. I can't think of one time she's mentioned a bucket list. No. In the end, she worries about what her absence will do to her patients and to her son, Spencer.

Each afternoon, I bring in the mail and drop another stack of letters, cards, and gifts, mostly from people I've never even met. Some are from previous patients who've healed from their cancer, and others are from the family members of those who've passed under Linda's care.

Once the letter count reaches five hundred, I stop counting and just put them in a large pile in the corner. After a few days, she struggles to sit up and read them on her own, so I sit on the bed and read each one aloud to her. Some are beautiful, hopeful things, while others are touching and rather sad. Reading twenty years' worth of love and gratitude from thousands of patients is somewhat cathartic for Linda. In no way will she ever understand the impact she's had on these people's lives, but in a way, I think it allows her heart to heal, despite her body refusing to.

I haven't reached my moment of catharsis yet, I think, watching Linda thumb through a dozen unopened cards beside her. I'm sure I will, but right now, I need to be strong for her. I'll have my time later.

With cancer, we are all in the same storm together,
but in a different boat.

When a person begins drowning, after they've inhaled a lungful of water, they tend to feel bodily peace. The mind realizes the struggle is over. Muscles have no strength left to fight. So, following the worst seconds of their life, time becomes suspended, and just before death, they experience a sense of calm.

Hospice isn't much different than that. Of course, that feeling of peace isn't constant, but the heaviness, the constant stress, the wishing and wondering what will be, is suddenly gone. No more choices to make, or battles to fight. The air around feels noticeably lighter, like the band around your lungs has snapped and you're able to take a full breath again.

Please hear me when I say cancer is not a death sentence. You might be
surprised to know many of my patients are still alive from 18 years ago
when my medical practice began. They are doing well, healthy, and
living their best life.

In these moments of peace, Linda and I sit together, facing one another on our opposing beds, holding hands. We laugh more in one hour than we have in the last year. Suddenly, nothing is off the table. When "death," the Voldemort[29] of words, becomes strangely commonplace, you allow yourself to discuss things you never would before. Silly, beautiful thoughts. Others, down-right funny.

I wonder how many times I've been the cause of that smile. Images from the last twenty years run through my mind. Sitting in the theater, mouthing every word to *Rent*. Standing in a forty-foot circle made of tiki-torches. Standing at the finish line at the end of each marathon drinking a beer. In the midst of my reverie, I'm struck by just how often those smiles are followed by an eyeroll. Now thinking through them all, one didn't happen without the other following immediately after.

"You know," I say, nudging Linda's arm, "one thing I think I'll miss the most are your eyerolls."

"My what? My eyerolls?" she asks, furring her brow. "What do you mean?"

"You know, when I inevitably do something stupid, and you just have to roll your eyes at me. It's my favorite indicator that I've done something wrong, and at the same time, something very right," I say, chuckling. She gives me a scowl, then rolls her eyes before realizing what she just did. "Hah! See?"

Suddenly, one of my fondest memories appears. One I haven't thought of in at least a year if not longer. I see it in perfect detail before me like a scene from a movie. It's from late November in 2013, when Linda and I were on a trip to New Orleans with our best friends, the Websters.

We were in a cab on our way to a restaurant called Commander's Palace, some fancy, hoity-toity place picked out by Linda and her best friend, Andrea. "You have to wear pants to this place," Linda said, gesturing to my shorts and sandals.

It was two o'clock on a Saturday afternoon, and the weather was perfect. "No, I don't. We're in New Orleans." I said, casually. "No one has to wear pants in New Orleans."

---

[29] Voldemort, a.k.a. "He who must not be named." I must have some *Harry Potter* fans reading this book.

She sighed, "Yes, Kermit, you do. And you have to wear a collared shirt."

I looked at Scott, whose eyes had grown a bit wide during this exchange between us. The look on his face practically shouted, "You better do what she says." I shrugged, unperturbed. "You don't wear pants in New Orleans." I said, then turned to look out the window. I could feel her eyes on me the rest of the drive, though she said nothing else.

We arrived at Commander's Palace shortly after. The hostess greeted us with a smile and said, "I have your reservation from three months ago. Your table is now ready for you," she gestured for us to follow, then stopped short. "However, this gentleman cannot be seated with you," she said, looking at me from the neck down. "He is not wearing appropriate attire."

The fire from my wife's eyes was now burning a hole right into my temple. I smiled politely at the hostess. "Is my wife looking at me right now?"

She smiled back with equal politeness, "Yes. Yes, she is."

"Would you please seat our party? I will be back in proper attire prior to the appetizers being served." Then without looking at my wife, I turned around and strode out.

It was pure dumb luck that there was a thrift store not two blocks away. I walked inside the store, strode right up to the lady behind the counter. "Hi. I told my wife I did not need pants and a collar for the restaurant that's down at the end of the block, but I do in fact, need pants and a collar. Now, I'm in trouble. You have to help me, and it doesn't matter how ridiculous it is."

Her face lit up like I'd just let her in on an inside joke. "Oh yes, I've been there before. Let me see what we got."

She had me dressed in less than four minutes, and for less than $8. I walked through the doors of Commander's Palace for the second time that afternoon, clad in a blue tight-fitting collared shirt with a design like that of a pirate's treasure map, and vintage pinstripe white baseball pants. And of course, open toed sandals.

The hostess did her best not to laugh as she spotted me at the entrance, then walked me to the table. Her expression was somewhere between horror and amusement. "Thank you," I said to the hostess. I spared a glance toward Linda who had put a napkin over her face, then to Scott, who cackled at me.

"Do not laugh in an establishment as fine as this. We have to conduct ourselves with proper etiquette," I said, keeping my face and tone quite serious. "When did the appetizers hit the table?" I asked to no one in particular. Andrea, who I know loved every damn minute of it, looked at me stoically and said, "three minutes ago."

"Honey," I said, turning to face Linda. "I'm sorry, I'm three minutes late." *Cue the infamous eyeroll.*

Though that memory always pissed her off, it still made her laugh every time we'd talked about it.

I smile. Even as she lay on the bed next me, in some of her final days, I still can't explain why I've always craved her eyerolls. It's been like a strange fetish for getting in trouble. Nothing ever lifted my spirits so much as when she looked at me with chagrin. And that's the way it had always been between us: We'd go somewhere, I'd forget to pack something important. I'd get yelled at, then I'd do something worse just to get yelled at some more. If only annoyance were an official love language.

But then, a thought hits me. My eyes go wide. She looks at me from her bed.

"What?" she asks, unaware of my recent trip down memory lane.

"Would you do me a favor? From here on out, whenever I really step in it, would you dim the lights wherever I am?" I ask, getting excited. "That's how I'll know you're giving me an eyeroll. Maybe just dim a lamp for the small stuff, but if the eastern seaboard goes out, I'll know I've really stepped in it."

She scowls for a second, then cracks, unable to hold it. Though softer than normal, her laugh still comes as more of a cackle. *Oh, how I'm gonna miss that sound.*

I'm going to miss the chemistry of our friends, too. Linda was the glue that held us together. Any time a trip needed to be executed, Linda was at the forefront of the planning. Hotels, transportation, packing... she did it all.

One note sticks out to me in, a message from a friend that captures the essence of our time together:

> *"I can truly say that our circle of family will never live life without love. What a blessing that is! You'll never be replaced in our lives - you'll be the constant reminder of our best and happiest times. Those memories will sustain us until we're together again. Love you forever ♥.*

Then just below, written to Linda specifically:

> *"'Do not pity the dead, Harry. Pity the living, and, above all, those who live without love.' — J.K. Rowling, and I cannot think of a more perfect way to say, 'See you soon' than this."*

"Do not pity the dead. . . Pity the living, and, above all, those who live without love." I read those lines over and over again. I have not lived a life without love. In fact, I've lived life with a love greater than most could claim for themselves. How on earth did I get so lucky with her?

A few moments later, Linda's dog, Jordan,[30] walks up to Linda and licks her hand. This dog, a Black Mouth Cur, could do no wrong in my wife's eyes, despite his tendency to sabotage my life any chance he could. He jumps on Linda's side of the bed, and I spring forward, about to push him off. "Hey! Get off, dog," I say, trying to protect Linda's stomach.

"He can check up on me if he wants to," she says, petting his ear, "What's the worst that could happen, I could die?"

So, Linda. "You know, I've been thinking we could have an Egyptian funeral for you. I think it would be quite fitting."

She looks at me, still petting Jordan. "What do you mean?"

I shrug, gesturing to Jordan whose eyes continue to watch me like I'm the threat to his master. "Well, he is *your* dog. He might have to take one for the team. Maybe he should go with you. You know, to see you through to the afterlife and beyond, or whatever."

"Oh, Kermit!" she says, laughing despite hugging Jordan an inch closer. "Promise me you'll take care of him."

Oh, Lord. "Um, honey. I can make you a lot of promises. But taking care of that," I say, pointing my finger at Jordan's nose, "is not one I will make."

"What? Oh, come on." She brings his face next to hers and looks at me. The dog looks just as mortified by this idea as I am.

"Yeah, nope. Not gonna happen. The words, 'I love you, Jordan,' have never come out of my mouth, and never will." I cross my arms. So does Jordan.

Three days later, I crack. Denying my wife is not something I've ever been willing to do, and I won't start now. So, through gritted teeth, I promise to sacrifice my sanity and my pride to take care of that dog. The grin she gives me makes it *almost* worth it.

---

[30] Named after Michael Jordan, of course.

This is what I want for you. You must navigate the seas physically, emotionally, and spiritually. This will serve you well and give you an authentic purpose day in and day out.

There is a certain closure from getting to say goodbye to someone days from their passing, knowing you'll never see them again. You're able to prepare your heart, even prepare the right words, for that moment. It's what I would call a luxury afforded to everyone *but* the people who need it most.

Each day, Spencer spends time with his mom, sitting on her bedside, telling her about his day. She combs back his hair, asking him questions about his team and his friends. I let them have that time to themselves. Partially to let Spencer have time with just his mom, but selfishly, because watching him hurts. It forces me to imagine what life will be like when it's just the two of us, and that is unthinkable. So I push away those encroaching thoughts, trying instead to exist minute by minute. Which is surprisingly achievable when all one does is eat and sleep.

Linda's godparents and extended family, who are unable to visit in person, get such closure by saying their goodbyes through Zoom calls. Her staff get their closure through in-person visits. But those around Linda each day know there won't be that luxury. No set time to prepare, to share a final word, or say your last goodbye. It's exhausting, and yet, it's an awareness that doesn't go away. Each time you walk away, you wonder if those will be the last words you ever say to them. The last laugh you'll ever hear. Or the last kiss you'll ever share.

God knows the plans He has for me ... and for you.

It's been a week and a half since Linda's TPN removal. No food, limited water. I continue to change Linda's dressings every four hours, though color isn't so much a concern as the added pain from infection. When she uses the restroom, which is less frequent each day, I pick her up from the bed and carry her to the bathroom since she can no longer stand by herself. My schedule has become her schedule. When she's uncomfortable, I adjust the pillows beneath her. When she sleeps, I sleep. Most evenings, I order food to the house for Spencer and me, though I don't have the appetite for much.

LeAnn visits every day now, which is helpful, but hurtful at the same time. Daily visits only start when the patient is getting close to the end.

It's been thirteen days. Linda sleeps mostly, while I either sleep next to her, or just rest my hand on her leg next to me. When she wakes from her nap, I pick her up to use the restroom. It takes no more effort than lifting a child. With her in my arms, I stand on the scale in front of the shower before easing her down. Then I put her back in bed, trying not to disturb the wound on her stomach, and wait for her to fall back asleep before returning to the bathroom. I stand on the scale, weighing myself.

Sixty-one pounds. She only weighs sixty...one...pounds.

I return to the bed, feeling cold. I lay behind Linda, resting my hand on her hip. It doesn't feel real beneath my hand. There's no muscle left, just a layer of skin thinly wrapped around bone. I think of the times I've placed my hands on those hips. Feeling their roundness, their warmth. The beautiful curves my hands knew so well.

The sharp bone now fitting strangely against my palm makes it hard to remember what they used to feel like. I try to recall memories of our nights spent together. All I get are flashes of intimate moments before they disappear, and no matter how desperately I try to recall them, like remnants from a dream just before waking up, they're just beyond reach. I lay in the dark, listening to my wife's slow breathing, and all I can feel is the absence of flesh on my wife's hip.

> *All attempts to understand God's Plan does nothing but minimize His Purpose. Our Creator did not give us the ability to answer the "why" questions.*

The next day, Spencer asks for one last video of his mom. I wish we would have thought to do it two weeks before. She would have felt so much more like herself. Like the badass she was.

I set my phone to record, letting Linda say things in the beautiful way only she can. She speaks to the Spencer currently sitting in the bedroom, and the Spencer living twenty years from now who might want to remember his mother's voice. She speaks of life lessons, offering future guidance and words of encouragement. And a promise to love him, always.

I don't watch the video once it's recorded. The woman saying goodbye to her son does not embody my wife. She is not frail or weak. Yet what gets captured on camera is a tangible reminder of the opposite.

> *The Bible says in 1 Corinthians 13:12 "We don't yet see things clearly. We're squinting in a fog, peering through a mist. But it won't be long before the weather clears and the sun shines bright! We'll see it all then, see it all as clearly as God sees us, knowing him directly just as he knows us!"* [31]*I find comfort in knowing my questions will be answered soon.*

On day fifteen, I'm wondering how she can still be alive. Her breathing changes. A pause between inhaling and exhaling, making it hard for Linda to speak. Each breath, you wait, counting the seconds in between, wondering when, or if, the next breath will come.

We sleep mostly, waking only to touch hands for a time. When I wake before her, I spend what time I can with Spencer, though I'm mostly distracted. One ear is with him, while the other is listening to my wife take her last breath no more than five thousand times.

> *If you pray, pray for my son and his continued development as a healthy teenager. My heart is heaviest for him.*

When she's not able to speak, I play her favorite music, singing softly the words to MercyMe's, "I Can Only Imagine." My thumbs stroke the loose skin covering her knuckles. "It's OK, honey," I whisper close to her ear as my forehead rests against her temple. "I never thought I could be, but I'm ready."

---

[31] The Message translation.

> *Also pray I get front row seats to a few UNC games.*
> *I'm guessing TV's won't be needed anymore.*

The song plays softly next to us, the voice singing of awe and glory and peace. I picture Linda, standing before Jesus. Healthy, strong, no longer in pain. And full of joy, dancing before him. "Linda, you can let go."

Heaven holds so many privileges we can't even conceive what our creator has in store for us.

With His Abundant Love and Grace,

As a reader, I invite you to listen to the following song with your eyes closed and heart wide open. This song was in my head moments after her passing.

CHAPTER 10

It's OK To Not Be OK

My wife, Dr. Linda Lee Farmer, passed away at 2:30 in the morning on February 15th after eighteen days in hospice. I'm sitting in the dark. As I hold Linda's hand, I have the thought that she will never hold mine back. It fills me with sorrow. An angry sorrow, full of cutting thoughts, both aimed at me and aimed at God. I demand answers. *Lord, why did she have to hurt at the end? Why couldn't you take me? She could have done so much more.*

My mind drifts to Spencer and how I'm going to tell him. It won't come as a shock—he saw the pants that wouldn't stay up and the robe that hugged his mom's frail body for the last two weeks. At least his mom's pain is finally over.

He wakes at my touch and walks with me to our bedroom. We sit together in the dark, sharing a new kind of grief. I text Nancy and LeAnn, knowing some protocol has to be followed but not caring beyond that. Not caring what I should do the next day. Eating, sleeping, talking. It all seems so far away.

Part of me has died; been crudely cut off like an amputation. Am I to simply keep on living? Get dressed, have conversations, make dinner for Spencer, all while knowing there's no Linda waiting for me? Somehow, I feel numb and in pain all at the same time, crying warm angry tears that roll down my chin, darkening my shirt. I don't wipe them away. I don't need to hold myself together anymore. At least, not at this moment, in front of Spencer. Let him see me grieve the love of my life, as he grieves for his mother.

This doesn't make sense. God, I know you are good. But it doesn't make any damn sense. She had so much more to offer the world than me. Why not me?! Tell me why.

I feel out of breath. I wait, listening, unsure if I really want the answer. It doesn't matter. He doesn't give me one anyway.

I walk Spencer up to his room, hearing Nancy and LeAnn shuffle across the floor of our bedroom. I want him to be away when they do what needs to be done. I wait for Spencer to fall back asleep, then curl up next to him.

Sitting in the dark, texting Nancy and a few others, the house doesn't look any different, and yet I know it is. When dawn comes, Spencer's eyes begin to open as the sunlight streams through the window. "Do you want to get away?" I ask.

He looks at me, one eye still closed, "What do you mean?"

"Let's leave, buddy. Let's leave town," I say, "just the two of us. You pick anything this side of Texas and we'll go for two or three days. Pick a city you'd like to see, and we'll—"

"Hawaii," he says, suddenly awake.

I give him a look, that says, "Yeah, that's not the correct side of Texas ... pick another city."

"Washington D.C." Spencer says, confidently.

"D.C., You're sure?" I ask, though feeling a bit lighter already. This will give both of us something to look forward to.

He pauses, deliberating between more cities, but he's as tired as I am and finally says, "Yeah, Washington D.C."

"Perfect," I say. Might be a bit chilly this time of year, but – eh, we'll be fine.

We find Washington D.C. to be an unexpectedly peaceful place to grieve (even while our shorts and t-shirts were being whipped by freezing northern winds). Here, we are invisible to others who don't know our grief.

We see the thousands of headstones at Arlington National Cemetery. Soldiers whose lives were unfairly taken, families who had to keep on living without them. It's strangely comforting to know our pain isn't unique. That it's been shared by thousands of families over the centuries. I find it both beautiful and sad. We spend a good amount of time there, reading the names and sitting in the silence of the lost, before finding our way to the park.

In front of us, an elderly couple walks side-by-side, holding hands. Without warning, curls of anger roil in my gut. I feel Linda's hand in my own and I'm ripped back into the reality I've managed to escape for a few hours. A terrible heat rises to my face. *That was supposed to be us. We were supposed to grow old together.*

Then a new wave of anger strikes, crashing into the first. Only this anger is towards myself. I struggle between hating those innocent people, envying them for having what we deserved, and in the same breath, hating myself for resenting something so beautiful and sacred. I take a few breaths, realizing my emotions are not as stable as I pretend they are. I look to Spencer, who's oblivious to my mental war. I put my arm around him. Spencer needs this. We walk back to our hotel to get ready for dinner. We're silent as we walk, and I don't attempt to fill it with conversation. Silence can be healing.

Grief and sorrow are strange and unpredictable. I selfishly wanted that elderly couple to know just how lucky they were. I wanted to yell that they had exactly what I lost. But that wouldn't change this feeling. This unbearable pain I wish could be puffed away like smoke.

After C.S. Lewis lost his wife to cancer, he made this observation about grief: "It doesn't really matter whether you grip the arms of the dentist's chair or let your hands lie in your lap. The drill drills on."[32] There is nothing I can do to lessen this pain. But God doesn't allow pain because he is cruel. He allows pain because he is just. I remind myself that one only hurts as much as they love. And I loved Linda with everything I had.

---

[32] Lewis, C. S. *A Grief Observed*. Harper, 2015.

We pull up to the house and sit in the car for a while, trying to keep the bubble of suspended reality from popping. We look at each other, knowing it has to pop eventually.

Getting away was the best decision we could have made. It allowed us to talk, and I mean, really talk. He shared his feelings, and I shared mine. It was everything we needed it to be.

I walk into our house and see on the desk in the mudroom, my wife's stethoscope. Somehow a representation of both life and death. It was practically an extra limb, so attached to Linda every hour of her day. Now, it's just an object to be put away somewhere. Never to be warmed by the skin of my wife's neck. Never to be used to listen to another patient's beating heart.

I walk past, allowing a numbness to push one leg in front of the other while Spencer follows behind me. I wonder if he feels the same; looking at his mom's things and feeling the weight of when they were last touched by her hands.

Her favorite blanket lays across the foot of the bed. The one she would put across her lap every time we sat together, and every time she fell asleep. So many items in the house cause pain when I see them. That damn dammit doll she used to hit against the table, now sitting by our bedside. I walk into our bathroom and that damn robe she refused to take off sits draped over the bathtub. I curse, seeing us sitting on the edge of the tub, razor in one hand, hair in the other, Nat King Cole singing "(I Love You) For Sentimental Reasons."

Dammit woman. I am never mad at you, and I never thought I could be, but why... WHY did you have to have hospice in our home? I can't look at the bed, our closet, the bathroom, or anything in this damn house without seeing you. Seeing you in pain, seeing you lose weight, seeing you smile despite everything.

I try to recall what it was like before. When it was just Linda and I, and a young Spencer, making cookies for Christmas, going to parties, marathons, soccer games ... but I can't. It's like a curtain that has been placed in front of every memory before the last ten months. All I can see is Linda's bandaged stomach and those hip bones.

The next day, I start planning Linda's funeral. She chose to be cremated, allowing Spencer and I some time, but time is now up. People will be expecting a beautiful service, and I intend to give it to them. I owe it to Linda's patients, our friends, and everyone else who loved her.

I reach out to Dr. George Mathison, a close friend and colleague of Linda's in her practice. He was also the pastor we met on our first day in Auburn twenty years before. In recommending Amsterdam Café, he solidified in Linda's mind that Auburn was to be our new home. I also reach out to Skip Long, a good pastor friend of mine who's a fraction less crazy than myself.

I sit at our kitchen table, thinking of how to possibly capture the essence of my wife through a service when Spencer sits down next to me. He watches me write some bullet points on a piece of paper before saying, "Hey dad, I'm going to talk at the funeral."

I look up. "What?"

"I am, and you're not stopping me." *Damn. His mom sure was Linda.*

"Son, that's a pretty big moment. Are you going to be ready for that?"

"If you're talking, I'm talking. I've got things I want to say," the offspring[33] says, his tone serious.

"There will be hundreds of people there, if not a thousand, brah."

"I can handle it."

"OK then," I say, not fully convinced, but I let it lie for now. Worst case, on the day, I'll just step in and read whatever he writes.

The next morning, I meet with Dr. George Mathison to discuss the service. We go over song choices, color schemes, and all the other items on my bullet point list. Then I lean across the desk and say sheepishly, "You know...when I get up to speak in your pulpit, I have to be honest. I must call my wife a badass. Because she was."

---

[33] Possible needed clarification: "offspring" is a term of endearment for me.

He smiles, his soft eyes crinkling as he nods, "She was, Kermit. She was. My pulpit is your pulpit."

We hold the funeral at Auburn United Methodist Church. Before the service, a few of Linda's closest friends string her cards together with a fishing line, decorating three of the four walls of the enormous sanctuary. As guests arrive, they walk around the room, reading the words of love and thanks addressed to their doctor and their friend. Spencer and I and other family members sit in the front row as each pew fills up with folks dressed head to toe in Carolina Blue. On the big screen, pictures throughout Linda's life are shown. Many see themselves in a few pictures and wonder about the origin stories of the others—400 pictures in total.

To start the service, Chris Kelsey, the director of worship (who became a close friend after) sings "I Can Only Imagine." His tenor voice does great justice to the song. I hear sniffling from the pews behind and see tissues being passed from friend to friend, despite them not even knowing the special significance behind the words being sung—The last time I heard this song, I was holding Linda's hand. We sang this song together no less than fifty times in those last eighteen days. I manage to keep the tears in check, telling myself I have a job to do. After the service, I plan to make myself available to Linda's patients, her staff, our friends, and anyone who has questions about Linda's passing. I owe it to them to not fall apart before then.

Strangely, I realize funerals aren't so much for the families as they are for everyone else. It's certainly not for the caregiver and those closest to Linda. Instead, it's for every person that's been touched in some way. A corporate love event. Those who love Linda need this opportunity to mourn our loss of her on this planet. They need this space to feel their love for her, then carry on with their regular lives. But for Spencer and me ... our healing must wait. Before we can dissolve into a blubbering mess, Spencer and I, as well as Brother Mathison, need to deliver the right message. The message Linda would want me to proclaim to her patients still fighting in their cancer journey. A message of hope, instead of sorrow.

The pianist finishes, and the audience applauses. I hear more sniffling from behind me as George Mathison walks to the podium. With his tender, resounding voice, he begins to speak about the wonder of my wife.

"Linda was more than a doctor, more than a leading specialist in her field of expertise. Her patients loved her, entrusted their lives to her;

and her love and care for them was unsurpassed, as many of you here today could so well testify. You all knew, and her other patients knew, she would never give up on them. She walked hundreds, nay, thousands of journeys down the cancer road. She knew their life stories, she knew their hopes and dreams, their fears and their hurts. They loved her, and she loved them. I believe Linda Farmer was the kindest person I've ever met. And Lord, if there's anything we need more of in this world today, it's more kindness. A soft and gentle kindness, as was found in Linda ... and the closer we are to Christ, the kinder we are to one another.

"A quality I greatly admired in Linda was, you always knew what she wanted, and where she stood. When I was visiting with Linda, she said to me, 'Brother George, will you officiate my funeral?' I said, 'Linda, I'll do anything in the world for you.' And with that sweet look upon her face, balanced by a firmness, she asked me a second time. 'George, will you officiate my funeral?' and I said, 'Linda, I'll do anything in the world for you.' Then Kermit, who can be firm too when he wants to be, looked at me and said, 'George, she wants a yes or a no out of you!' So, I looked at her, and I said the same words my sweet wife said to me when I asked her to marry me: 'Yes, yes, *yes!*'"

A swell of laughter erupts from the audience. I look at Spencer, who's smiling too. George then talks of Linda's capacity for love, using the Greek word, *Agape*, meaning a pure, sacrificial love that only desires what's best for others. *Oh, how accurate that is.* George then talks of her love for her precious dogs, and for her beloved North Carolina Tar Heels. He speaks of her love for her family, and for God. Then he shares one of my favorite memories with Linda:

"Only a physician could express love in these medical terms... When dating, Linda said to Kermit, 'I knew you first loved me, Kermit, when I saw your pupils dilate.'"

The crowd breaks again into giggles, smiling at one another in a knowing way. George continues:

"I tell you, only a doctor could say something like that. You may laugh, but for doctors, that is a very romantic term of endearment. Linda loved Kermit. And she loved Spencer, from the first moment she saw him. As Kermit shared with me, seeing Linda hold Spencer in that South Korean airport was the epitome of unconditional love."

Those last words he says while looking straight at me. I nudge Spencer's shoulder with mine, giving him a sideways smile. He gives me a smile back, and I lean over, kissing the side of his head.

"Now, when Kermit and I were planning this service, he asked me a question, one that I don't think we'll ever have the answer to. He asked me, 'Why?' Even Linda asked me: 'Why is my time now?' And I said, 'I don't have an answer, but I know God does not leave us in the dark about his intentions if we go to His word.' I read to her 1 Corinthians 13:12:

> *'Now we see things imperfectly, like puzzling reflections in a mirror, but then we will see everything with perfect clarity. All that I know now is partial and incomplete, but then I will know everything completely, just as God now knows me completely.'*[34]

"Brother Kermit, I believe that on Tuesday, February 15th, God dispatched one of his special angels to come down to a home on 8 Mile Road, and that angel gathered up the sweet soul of Linda, and winged its way back to Heaven, placing Linda in the tender and loving arms of the Lord Jesus. And I believe Linda heard him say, 'Well done, my good and faithful servant. You have been faithful over that which I have entrusted to you, as a faithful wife, a loving mother, a caring doctor. My child, enter now, into that which I have prepared for you. Hallelujah!'"

A resounding "hallelujah!" fills the sanctuary. I smile, feeling a tightness in my chest, my heart singing *hallelujah* right along everyone else. Spencer and I walk to the pulpit.

Emotions are warring in my head as I prepare to speak. On one hand, I'm focused on just keeping it together. I've been able to manage fairly well, considering. On the other hand, I have much to communicate. For one, when I look out at the crowd, I see so many of Linda's patients across the sanctuary, all there with a silent question in mind: *How did Linda, someone with a bullet-proof heart, succumb to the clutches of cancer, that villain she fought so hard to eradicate for over 9,000 patients in her practice? What does that mean for me?* So, my first mission is to do my best to answer that.

---

[34] The Message translation

But perhaps most importantly . . . *How many times can I get Linda to dim the lights?* I channel my inner pufferfish, take out my phone, and ask to take a selfie from the pulpit. "Go Heels!" someone shouts. *Surely that will get me an eyeroll from Heaven.*

I look at Spencer. It's his time to speak. I wait, wondering if the moment will be too much, but with chin up and back straight, he walks up to the podium. *Here we go. Keep it together Kermit.*

> "I came up here to say a few things about my mom. I knew her as a hard-working doctor, and a very determined mother. She was always there for me during the tough times, and I always had a shoulder to lean on. It hurts to see her go, but at least she's not in pain, and right before she left," he says, looking up at the crowd now, "she told me, 'Spencer, I will always be your guardian angel,' so that said, she will always be here with me."

An "amen," from someone in the audience is followed by a strong chorus of, "amen." Spoken with grace and poise. *Amen, son.* I kiss the side of his head before taking the pulpit. *Here we go, honey.*

"I don't think we should be sad. I don't think we should feel sorrow. We were the lucky ones. We're the ones that got to know her, the ones that got to experience her contagious smile. Hearing that clickety clack coming down the hallway. That clickety clack is at the house too; her motor just doesn't stop."

I laugh. Everyone in the room laughs too.

"We were lucky in that we got impacted by her life. As patients, you were impacted by her care. So, there's no need for sadness. What happened with my wife and the infections she got were very unique to her. When it comes to your own plight with cancer, just know that every plight is different. Those of you who've thought, 'If she were so strong and passed, how do I stand a chance?' Believe me when I say, 'Comparison is the thief of joy.' It is a fruitless road to walk down, and one Linda never did. There are more than 200 types of cancer.[35] Each cancer is different, and each person who has a type of cancer, has a unique combination of factors that change their battle. I look at the patients I know, connecting for a brief time with each pair of eyes looking at me, before continuing.

The love she had for you, as her patients, was unique. Linda spelled love, T-I-M-E.

I let that last word hang in the air. And I look at the patients I know, connecting for a brief time with each pair of eyes looking at me.

"She knew your medical history and as important, your personal history, your circumstances, your personalities. And all that time spent getting to know you made her love you even more. Think of one word that represents my wife, to you. Each of us has a word that's unique. For Brother George, it was 'gentle.' And I love that, because she was. A patient of hers might say 'believer,' because she practiced in a way that carried her faith into her career. For some, it's 'nurturer' or 'provider.'

Here, I chuckle inwardly, knowing what word I'm about to utter in front of a thousand folks inside the holy church.

---

[35] "Types of Cancer." Cancer Research UK, November 13, 2023. https://www.cancerresearchuk.org/about-cancer/what-is-cancer/how-cancer-starts/types-of-cancer.

"I call her my *badass*."

A few more words, then I ask the members of the Spencer Cancer Center to stand. I thank them for humbly and honorably carrying on my wife's legacy, devoting themselves to the kind of care she devoted her own life to. Then, I say something I'm not sure anyone expected. I say it, because I mean it, and because I need a reason to get out of bed tomorrow, and the next day and the next. I make a declaration to those in attendance:

> "As a care provider for the past ten months, I've noticed a few things. In over forty years of healthcare, there's been a tremendous amount of innovation, but that hasn't translated into a way to help patients in a quick and seamless way. The world is digital, but the engagement between doctor and patient is analog. That's something I'm very much interested in fixing. I'm going to tell my wife's story. I'm going to honor my wife by using my gifts and talents to improve the patient experience and patient journey going forward.
>
> "Now, I'm going to take this show on the road."

I walk off the stage, and Spencer hands me the first of several gifts along the front of the stage, wrapped in Carolina Blue and a white silk ribbon. I walk to Dr. Olivia Hall, the first female doctor Linda ever recruited, and gift her my wife's stethoscope. Then I find Dr. Lee Sharma, Linda's colleague and UNC bestie practicing GYN. "Don't open it here, it's gonna be an ugly cry," I say, handing her our UNC flag that's been in front of our house for years. "My wife would have wanted you to have that."

Then, I find Amy Baxter. Then Nancy, who knows what's in the box before I even hand it to her. She thanks me silently for Linda's robe. Not three months earlier, Nancy demanded that Linda, "Take off that damned robe and start living your life!"[36]

Then I find Sarah-the-Great, one of our at-home nurses. "Sarah, here you go," I say, handing her Linda's favorite blanket. Spencer whispers to me that it's the wrong person. I tell him no, that there are two women who have the same name but that are spelled differently, and that I got this. I laugh into

---

[36] Worth noting, it took Nancy over a year to even open the gift – much less wear it. She finally found the right time.

the mic, "Thank you fifteen-year-old who knows everything…" The crowd laughs as I continue to wander between the crowd.

Spencer hands me the last gift. It reads, "Sarah the Great."

Damn it. I was wrong. I expect the lights to dim at any moment now. Spencer tells me that's what he was trying to tell me the whole time. I hang my head, punching the air with the microphone, and say, "My wife loves to give me eyerolls. And that sure earned me an eyeroll from Heaven." I swap the gifts between the two ladies and beg for forgiveness.

Finally, I hand Linda's sister, Eunjoo, my wife's Korean bible, whose margins were filled with Linda's notes, thoughts, and observations. I kneel, leaning close. Away from the mic, I whisper in her ear, then leave a kiss on her cheek before Spencer and I take our seats once more.

Pastor Skip Long stands at the pulpit.

"Now, if it were up to me, or even Brother George Mathison, I think we'd have chosen to play 'Amazing Grace' or something like that. But that wouldn't work for Kermit," he says, giving a booming laugh. "This song we're about to play reflects the relationship between Linda and Kermit Farmer. It's about a man who tried his best to corrupt a pure and innocent heart."

If she isn't eyerolling now…

Pastor Skip continues, "Now, it may be worth noting that Kermit was unsuccessful in his attempts at corruption. He tried twenty years ago, and is still trying today, but is still unsuccessful. You may be wondering why. Spencer, you may be wondering why. So, I'll tell you why."

He pauses for just a beat.

"Your mom. Linda. She was the salt of the earth."

Dammit, I love that woman.

"And what the world needs now is a few more Lindas. Can I get an 'amen'?"

The crown shouts "Amen!"

"Now, this is where we're gonna act like this is my church ... I'm gonna need y'all to clap."

As the audience starts to clap, a song blasts through the speakers. Those who know the song start to laugh, clapping louder to Billy Joel's, "Only the Good Die Young," the only song that could possibly make sense of Linda's passing.

A few weeks after the funeral, Spencer and I are sitting in front of the TV. No one thought the UNC Tar Heels would make it to the Elite Eight, yet here we are, watching the Tar Heels play against Saint Peter's Peacocks. With popcorn in hand, we whoop and curse as the ball flies across the court.

Before she passed, Linda told me she would be the Tar Heels' guardian angel. I laughed at the time, but boy, do I believe her now. It's like she's there, guiding the ball in, or pushing the ball out, all at the exact right time. Then the final buzzer goes off.

Saint Peter's: 49

Tar Heels: 69

Against all odds, and everyone's expectations, the Tar Heels have just made it to the Final Four. I turn to Spencer. "Do you want to go?"

"Go where?" he says, still watching the TV.

I grab his shoulder, turning him towards me. "Do you want to go?" I ask again, looking from him, to the TV, then back, waiting for him to understand.

"Uhhh, what are you talking about?"

"Do you think Mom would want us to go to the Final Four?" I ask. He looks from me to the TV, then whoops again. I take that to mean "Hell yes!"

A week later, after clearing our calendars with Spencer's cousins, Andrew and Joanne Joung, our nerves are off the charts walking into the Final Four.

It's not just any game. It's a game that's never happened in the history of March Madness. UNC is up against Duke. The ultimate game of rivals. Linda told me time and again that if UNC ever played Duke on the big stage, she would be there to see it. And I still believe her.

The match is neck and neck. Everyone around us is swearing, jumping out of their seats, spilling drinks, crushing chips beneath their shoes, pulling on the necks of their jerseys. I look at Spencer who's loving every second of it. I am too. I stop looking at the score, knowing Linda is here, somehow guiding that ball in the basket and away from the basket, just as she had for the Elite Eight and the Sweet 16 before. I reach down and feel my cargo shorts lower pocket and pat the vial of Linda's ashes I'd put there before leaving the hotel. I haven't told Spencer yet, but we both know mom is here with us. Ashes or no ashes.

With Linda's guardianship, the Tar Heels score 81 to Duke's 77, and the crowd erupts in cheers, waving flags and hugging each other as confetti rains down from the rafters above.

Spencer is beaming. I'm beaming for him and for my bride. Blue and white confetti fall from the rafters, flying everywhere. I reach for his hand and press the small vial into his palm. He looks up at me, questioning. "Should we leave it here?" I ask. He looks down, realizing that I've had her in my pocket this whole time. He looks up at me smiling, "Yes."

I let him find the perfect place to put his mom's ashes. My pocket, now empty, still feels as if Linda is there. And she is, really. My palm lands on my chest, feeling the heart that belonged to her for over twenty years. Then I find Spencer and hug him tight, resting in this moment. It is everything we need it to be.

CHAPTER 11

"Who Lives, Who Dies, Who Tells Your Story?"

$\mathcal{S}$ on, what in the heck are you doing to that truck?"

"Don't worry about it," Spencer says from inside the cab.

I look at my GMC Sierra. In my eyes, it's still new. I'd taken perfect care of her for the last sixteen years so that one day, it would be a gift to my son. She was nearly the same age as Spencer, just three months shy. I was starting to regret my decision looking at the torn-out ceiling panel and the red spray paint cans next to the front wheel.

"Um," I say, "I'm going to worry."

"It's my truck," he says, annoyed now. "You gave it to me." Then using all the force of his seventeen-year-old muscles, he grips the carpet with both hands. I hear a ripping sound, followed by a loud pop, and cringe.

Prior to this, he'd removed the muffler, added a lift kit, installed an eight-foot antenna, stickers everywhere... I could go on. We currently have obnoxious mud tires stacked up in the garage. They are so big Spencer says, "I have to cut out the fenders to make them fit." It feels like watching my grandmother get a face tattoo, right in front of me.

"Are you sure you want to be doing that?" I say, after a flurry of sounds.

"I have YouTube," he says, as if it were the same as being a certified car mechanic. "I'm making a starlight roof by running fiber optics through the ceiling—350 of them."

My poor girl…there's nothing I can do. *At least he's occupied,* I tell myself. At least he's doing something that makes him happy, and becoming an Asian redneck is healthier than some other decisions he could be making. I walk back into the house, check the time, then get on my computer to check in with the team. We've been waiting to hear back from a few clients.

Using my wife's insurance money, I started a company. Our value proposition and product speak to the heart of doctors, patients, and caregivers alike by, "Helping patients to navigate the complexity of healthcare, one step at a time." One of our potential clients is the National Institute of Health (NIH) whose needs I'm hoping we can meet through a partnership and case study.

A few minutes later, I hear the garage door open, and the soft click of the door behind me. "Are you done giving my girl a not-so-beautiful facelift, son?" No response. I turn and he's leaning against the door frame, fiddling with a socket wrench. "Everything OK?"

"I wish mom could see the truck. I think she would've liked it."

I see Linda, shining from my memory, wearing the look of a proud mother. It's been nearly two years since I last saw that face; I can remember it better now than I ever could before. It takes time, but once grief morphs into a docile companion rather than a tyrannical dictator, your memories fade back into place, properly.

For months after the funeral, I couldn't remember what it was like to look at my wife and see the thriving, strong, badass doctor I'd been married to for nearly twenty years. Those eighteen long days in hospice robbed me of so much, and for a long time, I feared my true Linda would never come back to me. But God, grief, or maybe just the nature of our brains doesn't work like that. Eventually, time soaks up the pain like a sponge. Sometimes it gets so heavy, it dumps on you when you least expect it. Those days are hard. But then, for a little while, there's peace. And each time thereafter, the downpour gets lighter and lighter, until eventually, it's just a drizzle. A momentary melancholy cloud with brief flashes of subdued memories.

I picture Linda sitting in the front seat, equally exacerbated, but still marveling at her son's initiative and creativity, all the while scoffing at me for crying over some material thing.

"I think she would have liked it too," I say.

Spencer nods, then goes back to the garage, not saying anything. I realize, with pride, we haven't fought much this week. It feels a bit strange, actually. Like we've grown since our last fight. Or maybe, I have. He's seventeen. I don't expect him not to fight with me. I know he'll push me to get what he wants. He's still my son, a gladiator who eats nails for breakfast, just as his mother did.

I think back to our latest arguments, over the truck, money, his mom—it's hard to know what's right without her here. There used to be three people in every conversation, three people to cast votes. I always expected her to be there, to mediate when I was too stubborn or opinionated. Or, more precisely, I anticipated that I'd be the level-headed one while she'd be screaming, "You're Asian and you're *still* bad at math?!"

Shortly after the funeral, Spencer said to me, "I'm never going to win another argument again, am I?" I couldn't honestly argue with that point. It was all on me now. To know when to say no, when to ask forgiveness and when to forgive, when to be lenient and extend grace, or when to draw a hard line in the sand. In the last two years, I believe I've made more parenting mistakes than right decisions. Lord knows I'll make plenty more. And yet, each day comes a little bit easier. I know, on the inside, that every conversation does not have to be a teachable moment, though I find it hard not to share what I've learned through life experiences. No parent wants their child to make the same bone-headed decisions, and yet, sometimes life has to be the teacher.

At the very least, I want the offspring to wake up every day knowing a few things to be true. For one, I'd keep telling him that you can't change the past, but you can choose how you live out the future. So, despite how cliché it sounds, by this time, Spencer had heard these words from me:

"Spencer, I don't want you to waste time looking at the past thinking, *Why didn't I. . .?* Instead, wake up every morning and say, 'What I can do to change the future is...' If your mother loved anything, it was efficiency. It created happiness in her; she knew what she wanted in her life. Your path is your own. So how are you going to live out your life in honor of your mom?"

169

Unrelated, I'd also informed Spencer that I would have another highly successful romantic relationship. Of course, before she passed, Linda gave me this blessing in her funny Linda way: "A year from now, you can date someone, and a year from that, you can marry again."

So bluntly intentional. And yet, it was the kindest gift she could have bestowed on me. The gift of happiness, of a full life beyond hers. She knew what our marriage meant to me, and how, if it were up to me, that subject would never have crossed my mind while she breathed on this earth. But unlike me, Linda was never a selfish person. She would rather come back to haunt me until I found happiness, than let me live as if I were already dead.

Well, after nearly two years, I've yet to fulfill that promise. But who knows what God has planned.

It's complicated to make things really simple. And while I'm no technologist, I can leverage social capital. Two years ago, I called the Head of Experimentation of Capital One and said, "Ryan, put people in my life who can build this thing in my head. I'm calling the company Paths."

Doctors are burdened with knowledge that they have so little time to share, and it's too much to expect that patients will remember every word and detail of what the doctor is saying to them. Patients need the ability for their doctor to go home with them. Paths provides a solution for this. Paths is a series of steps that inform and guide both patients and family caregivers struggling to navigate our increasingly complex healthcare system. I saw the need for modern tools to communicate effectively and thoroughly with patients. Paths is a patient-centric model, streamlining patient onboarding, driving medical education, and dramatically improving both pre- and post-treatment outcomes.

At Paths, we're building the airplane as we fly it. What I know is my wife was a prolific educator to her patients. Now, I'm helping doctors be better educators in the limited time they have with their patients. Face-to-face and human-to-human interaction is so critical for effective care, and when patients lose those, they are left fearful, doubtful, and confused.

I'm not a healthcare guy or even an entrepreneur, and yet I've had to become both to reach what I'm really after. I feel like I've had to learn German to speak French. But in truth, I just want the problems Linda and other doctors like Wes have faced to go away. I want doctors to leave their practice every day knowing their patients are satisfied with their level of care. And I want patients to know they own the knowledge they need to take their next steps to recovery.

I don't believe Martin Luther King Jr. had a dream. In fact, I'll go even further. I call bullshit (before anyone gets offended at this, keep reading).

People have all sorts of dreams, and if they're lucky and if they have courage, they can choose to pursue those dreams. When pursuing your dream, you choose to wake up and stretch, make a cup of coffee, then sit down with a pen and paper, or whatever, and say, "I'm gonna work on my dream."

MLK was never afforded that luxury. He never had a dream. The Dream had him. It wasn't a choice to be considered or made. It was something deep within him that was worth dying for. A relentless pursuit that was against the odds of probability, but that didn't matter. He knew what he signed up for.

What I have deep inside me, is to rebuild the doctor-patient relationship, which is a different Dream than the one that gripped MLK. It's different than the one that obsessed the Wright Brothers'. It's not the same one that fueled Mother Teresa's quest to serve the sick. But perhaps it's equally as powerful.

When the Dream has you, instead of you having a dream, it's bigger, it's stronger. It rips you out of dead sleep at 2 o'clock in the morning, like a puppet put into motion, controlled not by your own desires but the Dream itself. When the Dream has you, you're not always the one making the plans, or even captain of the ship; sometimes, you're the passenger. It doesn't matter if your back muscles are screaming at you to stop, or your arms are so tired that you don't believe you can keep rowing; you go on simply because you must.

I don't speak from a place of bitterness or even grief. Not anymore at least. Rather, I see it as a calling, a mission, a relentless pursuit. When someone asks me why I work so hard to improve the patient journey and experience, and in the same breath, says how great it is that I have the heart for such work, that it's so amazing I'm able to *follow my dream* ... All I think is, *If I could pursue my dream, it'd involve a hammock on some beach, a food truck, and an ice-cold Corona in my hand.*

My wife's life and legacy birthed a thing in me that cannot be ignored. The torch she spent twenty years cultivating, I will carry. I carry without joy, without fear, without happiness, without any emotion really. I carry it because I must. With honor and with full acceptance. I'm thankful for this role I play. It tells me why I wake up every morning.

"I thought I could describe a state; make a map of sorrow. Sorrow, however, turns out to be not a state but a process . . . . Grief is like a long valley, a winding valley where any bend may reveal a totally new landscape." - C.S. Lewis, *A Grief Observed*

To her last day, my wife trusted in God's will. Her faith was always stronger than mine. Her knowledge of the Bible too. When a patient passed unexpectedly, she never raged against God, claiming it wasn't their time, or blamed herself for their death. Instead, she'd pray with distraught family members. She'd say to them, "They are at peace now. There's no more pain, only joy in Heaven."

My wife lived with pain as someone who lives with asthma: an unfortunate but permanent fact of life. It wasn't always the physical kind of pain, though she became all too acquainted with that in the end. And yes, there was the empathetic kind of watching others who were in pain. But what Linda experienced each day came from withholding nothing. Not her mind or her body, and certainly not her heart. To love as fiercely as my Wonder Woman loved her patients, was to know the kind of love Jesus felt, dying on the cross, sacrificing his own life to save others.

I know Linda Lee was not an angel, nor was she perfect in any sense of the word. She lacked patience, couldn't cook, insisted on excellence, and swore like a sailor upon occasion. But when her life got stripped down to the bone, emotionally and physically, she surrendered. There was no fear, only faith. Faith that she had carried out her mission on earth, to bring the love of Jesus to her patients, no matter the cost. And she found peace in that.

In 1 Corinthians 13:12, Paul wrote:

"Now we see things imperfectly, like puzzling reflections in a mirror, but then we will see everything with perfect clarity. All that I know now is partial and incomplete, but then I will know everything completely, just as God now knows me completely."[37]

I am not like my wife, not by a long shot. Just after my wife passed, I didn't care what Paul had said about God's unknown plans, or the perfect clarity He would someday give me. Instead, I cursed at Him, up, down, and sideways for taking my Linda away from me. For taking Linda *instead* of me. I felt inadequate, angry, useless. Life held nothing for me, and I couldn't even want the peace my wife found in the end. I was in too much pain. But God redeems pain the same way he reveals His will: slowly, with intention. It's OK to feel too much pain, to sit in that place where life means nothing, to think God has gone silent. That kind of pain came from twenty years of devoting my life to my wife. How could I have experienced anything less?

Now here I stand, nearly two years later, on a path that was thrust upon me against every hope, against every prayer. But there is one thing I know above all else. Good will come out of this. Not because grief is quick, or the path to healing is anything but straight, but because I mandate it. I declare it. There is no accelerated path to healing. It is a journey one must make on foot. Just as the Israelites wandered the desert for forty years, doubting the provision and the goodness of the God who brought them out of slavery, I was lost in the wilderness for a while. But God never abandoned me.

Today, my path to healing is not over, nor will it ever be. Much like the wound of my wife's stomach, the wound of my wife's passing will never fully heal. I've now joined a club alongside millions of others who've lost their spouse too early in life. No initiation, no signup bonus, just a membership that must be earned as each of us, in this new widow or widower role, finds purpose and meaning in tomorrow.

My future is to care for the caregivers which also includes the frontline of medicine personnel as they need more support and resources to accomplish their mission on a day-in and day-out basis. I accept this future as finite, just as Linda did in her profession and cancer journey. If my wife could find joy and grace, even in the face of death, I'd be at fault if I didn't do the same for the life ahead. I am no superhero, but a mere mortal, privileged to be in her

---

[37] The Message translation

presence for just over twenty years. She has made me the man I am today, and I am eternally thankful for her manifestation in me.

I accept that not all love stories have happy endings. Shah Jahan spent twenty-two years building the Taj Mahal to honor his late wife. It's one of the greatest love stories ever told. Elizabeth Schuyler Hamilton lived another fifty years after Alexander Hamilton passed. She told his story with passion, and over time, used her gifts and abilities to further his legacy. If it takes me twenty-two years, or even fifty, to manifest my love for Linda into something meaningful that outlives me, then so be it. The journey will have been worth it.

Linda would tell you medicine comes in many forms, but it begins with empathy and compassion. Be assured, Linda's love is still being shared, and good shall absolutely come from this tragedy.

I have a North Star for my journey ahead.

ACKNOWLEDGEMENTS

I have so many people to thank... alas... not all are represented here.

To Chris Kelsey, the professional rock in my life and the yin to my yang. You can't carry my weight but I'm thankful you carry me when needed.

To Tom and Vicki Hunt. I would not be who I am today without you and the gift and love you put into Linda. I don't have words to express my sincere thankfulness in guiding Linda, which in time guided me to become who I am.

To Joanne and Andrew Joung who help to keep me light-hearted and young.

To Skip and Andrea Long, your heart for service and community makes the world better, especially my world.

To my lefty bestie Anna Webster; it's been a real joy watching her grow from an infant into a young woman. Her father must remain nameless because he doesn't share his bourbon.

To Brandon Johnson for being there for my wife as a fellow oncologist and as her doctor. Linda wouldn't change a thing.

To John Christian, a surgeon with a compassionate heart. Thank you for the steadfast love you show all your patients.

To my Cancer Team Family at SCC, I love you as much today than prior to my wife's passing. The faces are new and ever-changing. You are still an extension of me and needed in my life today and going forward.

To "Sarah the Great", the home health nurse extraordinaire that will move mountains for her patients.

To Amy Baxter, Spencer's second mom and now first. Without you, I'm not sure what our family would have done to navigate the waters of life.

To Jeremy Davis, for believing in me and in the product of Paths. Thank you, my new friend.

To Barb Martin, a person who gave me so much encouragement in a moment I really needed it.

To Jon Florin, a steadfast fighter who brings much needed awareness and advocacy to stomach cancer.

To Dr. Lee Sharma, the first pioneer of the Path product, and my friend.

To Dr. Graves, for coming out of retirement to meet patient needs when Linda could not.

To Kyle Lauver and the Rhymetic team, for making the Path product HIPAA- and SOC2- compliant and for keeping me out of jail.

To Ryan Troll, the key person that has advised and hired the right technologist for our team to make the engine go.

To Alex Leon, our chief engineer. I think my dude codes in his sleep. You allow me to sleep at night with your steady hand at solid work.

To Kuki and the best beard on the planet, and not too bad of a coder.

To Roman, to whom I owe so much. Roman can get in my head and make something out of nothing. His skills are beyond reproach. Slava Ukraini! And you sir are a hero!

To Kayla for laughing, crying and wrestling through this book journey with me.

To Paul Fair for helping me to take a leap to write this book. Thank you for encouraging me to tell Linda's story in a formal way.

Lastly, to my oldest sister, Danna, who lost her husband to cancer three hours after I lost my wife. I learned how to be a caretaker from her. Her dedication and love to her husband and his seven-year fight with cancer was unmatched. The first honorary nursing degree should go to my sister. Her learning curve was so steep. Her caregiver journey started at the age of twelve when she raised me and my twin. She does it all with such gracefulness few will ever know.

ABOUT THE AUTHOR

Kermit Farmer is the widower of one hell of a doctor. This led him to collectively advocate for doctors, patients and caregivers. Today, Kermit is a social innovator and the founder of Paths. He created the company to leverage the power of human relationships through technology by helping patients to navigate the complexity of healthcare. Kermit draws upon an extensive background in logistics management through a NASA affiliate and Royal Caribbean International to make complicated processes simple to manage and understand.

Kermit strives to address complex social service systems by making it simple for individuals to access the resources they need in a timely manner, while documenting their engagement.

Kermit lives in Auburn, AL with his son, and dog. He's a mediocre t-ball coach and a less than mediocre soccer coach. Kermit believes in Life, Liberty, and the pursuit of Great Pizza.

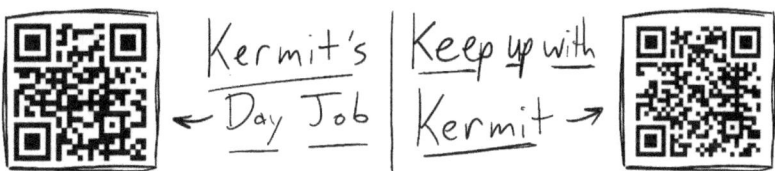

Kermit's Day Job ← | Keep up with Kermit →

A PATH FOR ALL

Dr. Linda Farmer had a passion for efficiency and being whatever her patients needed her to be . . . an adviser, an educator, a friend. After her passing in 2022, her dedication to providing the most thorough care possible for each patient was taken up by her husband, Kermit Farmer.

Through months of intense treatments and hospital admissions, Kermit became intimately familiar with the labyrinth that is our healthcare system. The challenges of this experience led to the inception of Paths, an online toolkit designed to complement the patient's physical experience. Physicians must communicate what they know as thoroughly as possible in an extremely limited amount of time, and patients and caregivers must retain this abundant information without sufficient resources ever being provided to them. Paths provides a solution.

Paths equips physicians and other medical care providers with engaging and uniquely efficient tools to communicate more thoroughly with their patients, while educating and guiding patients and family caregivers through diagnosis-specific content; it cost-effectively streamlines patient on-boarding, drives diagnosis education, enhances patient engagement and accountability, and dramatically improves both pre- and post-treatment outcomes. Paths creates a win-win environment between physicians and patients and aims to repair broken relationships caused by systems and practices that remove – intentionally or otherwise – the human component that is so essential to medical care.

Paths seeks to make a difference in the lives of patients and caregivers by putting the patient journey first.

WWW.VILLAGEPATHS.COM

Thank you for taking the time to be a part of our story. If you have any questions or thoughts, don't hesitate to reach out to Kermit at kermit@villagepaths.com.

www.ingramcontent.com/pod-product-compliance
Lightning Source LLC
Chambersburg PA
CBHW061137120626
46546CB00005B/2092